TCP/IP Sockets in C#

Practical Guide for Programmers

The Morgan Kaufmann Practical Guides Series

Series Editor: Michael J. Donahoo

TCP/IP Sockets in C#: Practical Guide for Programmers
David Makofske, Michael J. Donahoo, and Kenneth L. Calvert

Java Cryptography Extensions: Practical Guide for Programmers
Jason Weiss

JSP: Practical Guide for Java Programmers
Robert J. Brunner

JSTL: Practical Guide for JSP Programmers
Sue Spielman

Java: Practical Guide for Programmers
Zbigniew M. Sikora

The Struts Framework: Practical Guide for Java Programmers
Sue Spielman

Multicast Sockets: Practical Guide for Programmers
David Makofske and Kevin Almeroth

TCP/IP Sockets in Java: Practical Guide for Programmers
Kenneth L. Calvert and Michael J. Donahoo

TCP/IP Sockets in C: Practical Guide for Programmers
Michael J. Donahoo and Kenneth L. Calvert

JDBC: Practical Guide for Java Programmers
Gregory D. Speegle

For further information on these books and for a list of forthcoming titles,
please visit our website at *http://www.mkp.com/practical*

TCP/IP Sockets in C#

Practical Guide for Programmers

David B. Makofske

Akamai Technologies

Michael J. Donahoo

Baylor University

Kenneth L. Calvert

University of Kentucky

ELSEVIER

AMSTERDAM • BOSTON • HEIDELBERG • LONDON
NEW YORK • OXFORD • PARIS • SAN DIEGO
SAN FRANCISCO • SINGAPORE • SYDNEY • TOKYO

Morgan Kaufmann is an imprint of Elsevier

MORGAN KAUFMANN PUBLISHERS

Senior Editor	Rick Adams
Associate Editor	Karyn Johnson
Publishing Services Manager	Simon Crump
Project Manager	Kyle Sarofeen
Cover Design	Yvo Niezebos Design
Cover Image	Getty Images
Composition	Cepha Imaging Pvt. Ltd.
Copyeditor	Harbour Fraser Hodder
Proofreader	Jacqui Brownstein
Indexer	Michael Ferreira
Interior printer	Maple Press
Cover printer	Phoenix Color

Morgan Kaufmann Publishers is an imprint of Elsevier.
500 Sansome Street, Suite 400, San Francisco, CA 94111

This book is printed on acid-free paper.

Library of Congress Cataloging-in-Publication Data
Application submitted.

ISBN-13: 978-0-12-466051-9
ISBN-10: 0-12-466051-7

For information on all Morgan Kaufmann publications,
visit our Web site at *www.mkp.com*

Printed in the United States of America
08 07 06   5 4 3

For Margie and Jacob, for their love and inspiration
–David

For my three girls: Lisa, Michaela, and Mackenzie
–Jeff

For my parents, Paul and Eleanor Calvert
–Ken

Contents

Preface

For years, college courses in computer networking were taught with little or no "hands on" experience. For various reasons, including some good ones, instructors approached the principles of computer networking primarily through equations, analyses, and abstract descriptions of protocol stacks. Textbooks might include code, but it was unconnected to anything students could get their hands on. Perhaps in an ideal world this would suffice, but we believe that students learn better when they can see (and then build) concrete examples of the principles at work. Fortunately, such examples abound today. The Internet has become a part of everyday life, and access to its services is readily available to most students (and their programs).

The *Berkeley Sockets interface*, known universally as "sockets" for short, is the de facto standard application programming interface (API) for networking, spanning a wide range of operating systems. The sockets API was designed to provide *generic* access to interprocess communication services that might be implemented by whatever protocols were supported on a particular platform—IPX, Appletalk, TCP/IP, and so on. As a consequence of this generic approach the sockets API may appear dauntingly complicated at first. But, in fact, the basics of network programming using the Internet (TCP/IP) protocols are not difficult. The sockets interface has been around for a long time—at least in "Internet time"—but it is likely to remain important for the foreseeable future.

We have written this book to improve the support for socket-based programming exercises in our own networking courses. Although some networking texts deal with network programming, we know of none that cover TCP/IP sockets. Excellent reference books on TCP/IP socket programming exist, but they are too large and comprehensive to be considered as a supplement to a networking text. Our goal, therefore, is to provide a gentle introduction, and a handy reference, that will allow students to dive right in without too much handholding.

Enabling students to get their hands on real network services via the sockets interface has several benefits. First, for a surprising number of people, socket programming is their first exposure to concrete realizations of concepts previously seen only in the abstract. Dealing with the very real consequences of messy details, such as the layout of data structures in memory, seems to trigger a kind of epiphany in some students, and this experience has consequences far beyond the networking course. Second, we find that students who understand how application programs *use* the services of TCP/IP generally have an easier time grasping the principles of the underlying protocols that *implement* those services. Finally, basic socket programming skills are a springboard to more advanced assignments, which support learning about routing algorithms, multimedia protocols, medium access control, and so on.

Intended Audience

This book is aimed primarily at students in introductory courses in computer networks, either upper-level undergraduate or graduate. It is intended as a supplement, to be used with a traditional textbook, that should explain the problems and principles of computer networks. At the same time, we have tried to make the book reasonably self-contained (except for the assumed background) so that it can also be used, for example, in courses on operating systems or distributed computing. We have purposely limited the book's coverage in order to keep its price low enough to be reasonable for a supplementary text for such a course. An additional target audience consists of practitioners who know some C# and want to learn sockets. This book should take you far enough that you can start experimenting and learning on your own.

We assume basic programming skills and experience with C# and Microsoft Windows. You are expected to be conversant with C# concepts such as classes, methods, interfaces, and basic inheritance. We assume that you have access to a Microsoft Windows OS that can install and run the .NET Framework Software Development Kit (SDK)[1] and has access to the Internet (or some other TCP/IP network). The .NET SDK is a free download available at *www.microsoft.com/net*. This book uses version 1.1 of the .NET Framework, although the code should also work with version 1.0. Most of our examples involve compiling and running programs from a DOS command line; we assume that you can deal with that, although Microsoft Visual Studio may be used as well.

---

[1] If you prefer UNIX, there is also an open source implementation of the .NET development framework called Mono in the works. See *www.go-mono.com* for details.

Approach

Chapter 1 provides a general overview of networking concepts. It is not, by any means, a complete introduction but rather is intended to allow readers to synchronize with the concepts and terminology used throughout the book. Chapter 2 introduces the mechanics of simple clients and servers; the code in this chapter can serve as a starting point for a variety of exercises. Chapter 3 covers the basics of message construction and parsing. The reader who digests the first three chapters should in principle be able to implement a client and server for a given (simple) application protocol. Chapter 4 then deals with techniques that are necessary when building more sophisticated and robust clients and servers. Finally, in keeping with our goal of illustrating principles through programming, Chapter 5 discusses the relationship between the programming constructs and the underlying protocol implementations in somewhat more detail.

Our general approach introduces programming concepts through simple program examples accompanied by line-by-line commentary that describes the purpose of every part of the program. This lets you see the important objects and methods as they are used in context. As you look at the code, you should be able to understand the purpose of each and every line of code.

Our examples do not take advantage of all library facilities in the .NET framework. The .NET library includes hundreds of classes that can be used for networked applications that are beyond the scope of this book. True to its name, this book is about TCP/IP sockets programming, and it maintains a tight focus on the socket-related classes of .NET. Likewise, we do not cover raw sockets programming or sockets programming using protocols other than TCP/IP. We do not include the `WebRequest` and `WebResponse` classes, or any of the `System.Web` classes. We believe that once you understand the principles, using these convenience classes will be straightforward. The network-relevant classes that we do cover include `IPAddress`, `Dns`, `TcpClient`, `TcpListener`, `UdpClient`, `Socket`, and their associated enumeration and helper classes.

We include brief API summaries of the .NET classes discussed for convenience, but these are not complete summaries. Also, since .NET is relatively new and evolving, the reader is encouraged to utilize the full library reference on the Microsoft Developer Network website at *msdn.microsoft.com/library* for detailed descriptions, examples, and updates.

This book is not an introduction to C# or the .NET framework. We expect that the reader is already acquainted with the language and basic .NET libraries (especially I/O), and knows how to develop programs in C#. All the examples in this book are not necessarily production-quality code. Although we strive for robustness, the primary goal of our code examples is to educate. In order to avoid obscuring the principles with large amounts of error-handling code, we have sacrificed some robustness for brevity and clarity. We do not catch every exception that could occur, and in most cases we only catch exceptions that are particular to a class we are describing or a specific example we are trying to illustrate.

Similarly, in order to avoid cluttering the examples with extraneous (nonsocket-related programming) code, we have made them command-line based. While the book's website (*www.mkp.com/practical/csharpsockets*) contains an example of a GUI-enhanced network application, we do not include it or explain it in the text.

Acknowledgments

We would like to thank all the people who helped make this book a reality. Despite the book's brevity, many hours went into reviewing the original proposal and the draft, and the reviewers' input has significantly shaped the final result.

First, thanks to those who meticulously reviewed the draft of the text and made suggestions for improvement. These include (in alphabetical order): Durgaprasad Gorti, Microsoft Corporation; Adarsh Khare, Microsoft Corporation; Mauro Ottaviani, Microsoft Corporation; and Dev Subramanian, Chalmers University of Technology. Any errors that remain are, of course, our responsibility. We are very interested in weeding out such errors in future printings, so if you find one, please send email to any of us. We will maintain an errata list on the book's Web page.

Finally, we are grateful to the folks at Morgan Kaufmann, especially our editor Karyn Johnson and project manager Mamata Reddy.

For Further Information

This book has a website (*www.mkp.com/practical/csharpsockets*) that contains additional information, including all the source code presented in the book and errata. From time to time, we may also place new material on the website. We encourage you to take advantage of this resource, and to send us your suggestions for improvement of any aspect of this book. You can send feedback via the website maintained by the publisher, or you can send us email to the addresses below.

David B. Makofske   david_makofske@yahoo.com

Michael J. Donahoo   jeff_donahoo@baylor.edu

Kenneth L. Calvert   calvert@netlab.uky.edu

chapter **1**

Introduction

Millions of computers all over the world are now connected to the worldwide network known as the Internet. The Internet enables programs running on computers thousands of miles apart to communicate and exchange information. If you have a computer connected to a network, you have undoubtedly used a Web browser—a typical program that makes use of the Internet. What does such a program do to communicate with others over a network? The answer varies with the application and the operating system (OS), but a great many programs get access to network communication services through the "sockets" application programming interface (API). The goal of this book is to get you started writing programs that use the sockets API.

Before delving into the details of the API, it is worth taking a brief look at the big picture of networks and protocols to see how an application programming interface for TCP/IP fits in. Our goal here is *not* to teach you how networks and TCP/IP work—many fine texts are available for that purpose [2, 4, 10, 15, 20]—but rather to introduce some basic concepts and terminology.

1.1 Networks, Packets, and Protocols

A computer network consists of machines interconnected by communication channels. We call these machines *hosts* and *routers*. Hosts are computers that run applications such as your Web browser, the application programs running on hosts are really the users of the network. Routers are machines whose job is to relay or *forward* information from one communication channel to another. They may run programs but typically do not run application programs. For our purposes, a *communication channel* is a means of conveying sequences of bytes from one host to another; it may be a broadcast technology like Ethernet, a dial-up modem connection, or something more sophisticated.

Routers are important simply because it is not practical to connect every host directly to every other host. Instead, a few hosts connect to a router, which connects to other routers, and so on to form the network. This arrangement lets each machine get by with a relatively small number of communication channels; most hosts need only one. Programs that exchange information over the network, however, do not interact directly with routers and generally remain blissfully unaware of their existence.

By *information* we here mean a sequences of bytes that are constructed and interpreted by programs. In the context of computer networks these byte sequences are generally called *packets*. A packet contains control information that the network uses to do its job and sometimes also includes user data. An example is information about the packet's destination. Routers use such control information to figure out how to forward each packet.

A *protocol* is an agreement about the packets exchanged by communicating programs and what they mean. A protocol tells how packets are structured—for example, where the destination information is located in the packet and how big it is—as well as how the information is to be interpreted. A protocol is usually designed to solve a specific problem using given capabilities. For example, the Hypertext Transfer Protocol (HTTP) solves the problem of transferring hypertext objects between servers where they are stored and Web browsers that make them available to human users.

Implementing a useful network requires that a large number of different problems be solved. To keep things manageable and modular, different protocols are designed to solve different sets of problems. TCP/IP is one such collection of solutions, sometimes called a *protocol suite*. It happens to be the suite of protocols used in the Internet, but it can be used in stand-alone private networks as well; henceforth when we say "the network," we mean any network that uses the TCP/IP protocol family. The main protocols in the TCP/IP family are the Internet Protocol (IP), the Transmission Control Protocol (TCP), and the User Datagram Protocol (UDP).

It turns out to be useful to organize protocols in a family into *layers*; TCP/IP and virtually all other protocol families are organized this way. Figure 1.1 shows the relationships among the protocols, applications, and the sockets API in the hosts and routers, as well as the flow of data from one application (using TCP) to another. The boxes labeled TCP, UDP, and IP represent implementations of those protocols. Such implementations typically reside in the operating system of a host. Applications access the services provided by UDP and TCP through the sockets API. The arrow depicts the flow of data from the application, through the TCP and IP implementations, through the network, and back up through the IP and TCP implementations at the other end.

In TCP/IP, the bottom layer consists of the underlying communication channels, such as Ethernet or dial-up modem connections. Those channels are used by the *network layer*, which deals with the problem of forwarding packets toward their destination (i.e., what routers do). The single network layer protocol in the TCP/IP family is the Internet Protocol; it solves the problem of making the sequence of channels and routers between any two hosts look like a single host-to-host channel.

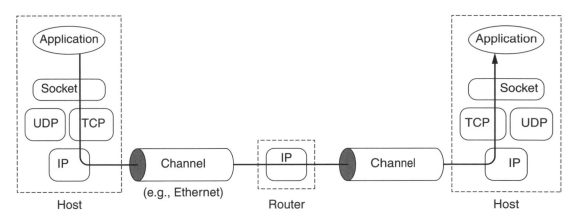

Figure 1.1: A TCP/IP network.

The Internet Protocol provides a *datagram* service: Every packet is handled and delivered by the network independently, like telegrams or parcels sent via the postal system. To make this work, each IP packet has to contain the *address* of its destination, just as every package you mail is addressed to somebody. (We'll say more about addresses shortly.) Although most parcel delivery companies guarantee delivery of a package, IP is only a best-effort protocol: It attempts to deliver each packet, but it can (and occasionally does) lose, reorder, or duplicate packets in transit through the network.

The layer above IP is called the *transport layer.* It offers a choice between two protocols: TCP and UDP. Each builds on the service provided by IP, but they do so in different ways to provide different kinds of channels, which are used by *application protocols* with different needs. TCP and UDP have one function in common: addressing. Recall that IP delivers packets to hosts; clearly, a finer granularity of addressing is needed to get a packet to a particular application, perhaps one of many using the network in the same host. Both TCP and UDP use addresses called *port numbers* so that applications within hosts can be identified. They are called *end-to-end transport* protocols because they carry data all the way from one program to another (whereas IP carries data from one host to another).

TCP is designed to detect and recover from the losses, duplications, and other errors that may occur in the host-to-host channel provided by IP. TCP provides a *reliable byte-stream* channel, so that applications don't have to deal with these problems. It is a *connection-oriented* protocol: Before using it to communicate, two programs must first establish a TCP connection, which involves completing an exchange of *handshake messages* between the TCP implementations on the two communicating computers. Using TCP is similar to file input/output (I/O). In fact, a file that is written by one program and read by another is a reasonable mode of communication over a TCP connection. UDP, on the other hand, does not attempt to recover from errors experienced by IP; it simply extends the IP best-effort datagram service so that it works between applications programs instead of between hosts. Thus, applications that use UDP must be prepared to deal with losses, reordering, and so on.

1.2   About Addresses

When you mail a letter, you provide the address of the recipient in a form that the postal service can understand. Before you can talk to somebody on the phone, you must supply their number to the telephone system. In a similar way, before a program can communicate with another program, it must tell the network where to find the other program. In TCP/IP, it takes two pieces of information to identify a particular program: an *Internet address*, used by IP, and a *port number*, the additional address interpreted by the transport protocol (TCP or UDP).

Internet addresses are 32-bit binary numbers.[1] In writing down Internet addresses for human consumption (as opposed to using them inside applications), we typically show them as a string of four decimal numbers separated by periods (e.g., 10.1.2.3); this is called the *dotted-quad* notation. The four numbers in a dotted-quad string represent the contents of the four bytes of the Internet address, thus each is a number between 0 and 255.

Technically, each Internet address refers to the connection between a host and an underlying communication channel, such as a dial-up modem or Ethernet card. Because each such network connection belongs to a single host, an Internet address identifies a host as well as its connection to the network. However, because a host can have multiple physical connections (interfaces) to the network, one host can have multiple Internet addresses.

The port number in TCP or UDP is always interpreted relative to an Internet address. Returning to our earlier analogies, a port number corresponds to a room number at a given street address, say, that of a large building. The postal service uses the street address to get the letter to a mailbox; whoever empties the mailbox is then responsible for getting the letter to the proper room within the building. Or consider a company with an internal telephone system: To speak to an individual in the company, you first dial the company's main number to connect to the internal telephone system, and then dial the extension of the particular telephone of the individual you wish to speak with. In these analogies, the Internet address is the street address or the company's main number, whereas the port corresponds to the room number or telephone extension. Port numbers are 16-bit unsigned binary numbers, so each one is in the range of 1 to 65,535 (0 is reserved).

---

[1] Throughout this book the term *Internet address* refers to the addresses used with the current version of IP, which is version 4 [11]. Because it is expected that a 32-bit address space will be inadequate for future needs, a new version of IP has been defined [5]; it provides the same service but has much bigger Internet addresses (128 bits). IPv6, as the new version is known, has not been widely deployed; the sockets API will require some changes to deal with its much larger addresses [6]. The .NET framework does support IPv6 addresses, but they are not covered in this book.

1.3 About Names

Most likely you are accustomed to referring to hosts by *name* (e.g., host.example.com). However, the Internet protocols deal with numerical addresses, not names. You should understand that the use of names instead of addresses is a convenience feature that is independent of the basic service provided by TCP/IP—you can write and use TCP/IP applications without ever using a name. When you use a name to identify a communication endpoint, the system has to do some extra work to *resolve* the name into an address.

This extra step is often worth it, for a couple of reasons. First, names are generally easier for humans to remember than dotted-quads. Second, names provide a level of indirection, which insulates users from IP address changes. During the writing of this book, the Web server for the publisher of this text, Morgan Kaufmann, changed Internet addresses from 213.38.165.180 to 129.35.78.178. However, because we refer to that Web server as *www.mkp.com* (clearly much easier to remember than 213.38.165.180), and because the change is reflected in the system that maps names to addresses (*www.mkp.com* now resolves to the new Internet address instead of 213.38.165.180), the change is transparent to programs that use the name to access the Web server.

The name-resolution service can access information from a wide variety of sources. Two of the primary sources are the *Domain Name System* (DNS) and local configuration databases. The DNS [8] is a distributed database that maps *domain names* such as *www.mkp.com* to Internet addresses and other information; the DNS protocol [9] allows hosts connected to the Internet to retrieve information from that database using TCP or UDP. Local configuration databases are generally OS-specific mechanisms for local name-to-Internet address mappings. Microsoft Windows provides a *hosts* text file where IP-to-domain-name mappings can be hard-coded or overridden. UNIX-based systems typically have a file called /etc/hosts that does the same thing.

1.4 Clients and Servers

In our postal and telephone analogies, each communication is initiated by one party, who sends a letter or dials a telephone call, while the other party responds to the initiator's contact by sending a return letter or picking up the phone and talking. Internet communication is similar. The terms *client* and *server* refer to these roles: The client program initiates communication, while the server program waits passively for and then responds to clients that contact it. Together, the client and server compose the *application*. The terms *client* and *server* are descriptive of the typical situation in which the server makes a particular capability—for example, a database service—available to any client that is able to communicate with it.

Whether a program is acting as a client or server determines the general form of its use of the sockets API to communicate with its *peer*. (The client is the peer of the server and vice versa.) Beyond that, the client-server distinction is important because *the client needs to know the server's address and port initially*, but not vice versa. With the sockets

API, the server can, if necessary, learn the client's address information when it receives the initial communication from the client. This is analogous to a telephone call—in order to be called, a person does not need to know the telephone number of the caller. As with a telephone call, once the connection is established, the distinction between server and client disappears.

How does a client find out a server's IP address and port number? Usually, the client knows the name of the server it wants, for example, from a Universal Resource Locator (URL) such as *http://www.mkp.com*, and uses the name resolution service to learn the corresponding Internet address.

Finding a server's port number is a different story. In principle, servers can use any port, but the client must be able to learn what it is. In the Internet, there is a convention of assigning *well-known port numbers* to certain applications. The Internet Assigned Number Authority (IANA) oversees this assignment. For example, port number 21 has been assigned to the File Transfer Protocol. When you run an FTP client application, it tries to contact the FTP server on that port by default. A list of all the assigned port numbers is maintained by the numbering authority of the Internet (see *www.iana.org/assignments/portnumbers*).

There are also numerous standards, protocols, and proposals for *directory services*, by which a client can query the services and locations available from servers from a directory. Of course, the client must know the address and port to contact the directory services server on in order to find this information! Again, this is typically defined and published as being at a "well-known" location for the intended clients.

1.5 What Is a Socket?

A *socket* is an abstraction through which an application may send and receive data, in much the same way as an open file allows an application to read and write data to stable storage. A socket allows an application to "plug in" to the network and communicate with other applications that are also plugged in to the same network. Information written to the socket by an application on one machine can be read by an application on a different machine, and vice versa.

Different types of sockets correspond to different underlying protocol suites and different stacks of protocols within a suite. This book deals only with the TCP/IP protocol suite. The main types of sockets in TCP/IP today are *stream sockets* and *datagram sockets*. Stream sockets use TCP as the end-to-end protocol (with IP underneath) and thus provide a reliable byte-stream service. Datagram sockets use UDP (again, end-to-end with IP underneath) and thus provide a best-effort datagram service that applications can use to send individual messages up to about 65,500 bytes in length. Stream and datagram sockets are also supported by other protocol suites, but this book deals only with TCP stream sockets and UDP datagram sockets. A TCP/IP socket is uniquely identified by an Internet address, an end-to-end protocol (TCP or UDP), and a port number. As you proceed, you will encounter several ways for a socket to become bound to an address.

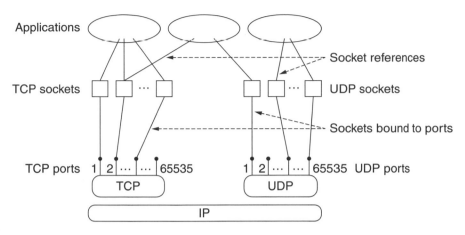

Figure 1.2: Sockets, protocols, and ports.

Figure 1.2 depicts the logical relationships among applications, socket abstractions, protocols, and port numbers within a single host. Note that a single socket abstraction can be referenced by multiple application programs. Each program that has a reference (called a *descriptor*) to a particular socket can communicate through that socket. Earlier we said that a port identifies an application on a host. Actually, a port identifies a socket on a host. Figure 1.2 shows that multiple programs on a host can access the same socket. In practice, separate programs that access the same socket would usually belong to the same application (e.g., multiple copies of a Web server program), although in principle they could belong to different applications.

1.6 Exercises

1. Can you think of a real-life example of communication that does not fit the client-server model?

2. To how many different kinds of networks is your home connected? How many support two-way communication?

3. IP is a best-effort protocol, requiring that information be broken down into datagrams, which may be lost, duplicated, or reordered. TCP hides all of this, providing a reliable service that takes and delivers an unbroken stream of bytes. How might you go about providing TCP service on top of IP? Why would anybody use UDP when TCP is available?

chapter **2**

Basic Sockets

You are now ready to learn to write your own socket applications in C#. One of the advantages of the C# programming language is its use of Microsoft's .NET framework, which provides a powerful library of APIs for programming. Among the class libraries provided are the System.Net and System.Net.Sockets namespaces, and most of this book is dedicated to how to use the socket APIs provided there. In this chapter we begin by demonstrating how C# applications identify network hosts. Then, we describe the creation of TCP and UDP clients and servers. The .NET framework provides a clear distinction between using TCP and UDP, defining a separate set of classes for both protocols, so we treat each separately. Finally, we discuss the Socket class that is the underlying implementation of all the higher level .NET socket classes.

2.1   Socket Addresses

IPv4 uses 32-bit binary addresses to identify communicating hosts. A client must specify the IP address of the host running the server program when it initiates communication; the network infrastructure uses the 32-bit *destination address* to route the client's information to the proper machine. Addresses can be specified in C# by their 32-bit long integer value or by using a string that contains the dotted-quad representation of the numeric address (e.g., 169.1.1.1). .NET encapsulates the IP addresses abstraction in the IPAddress class which can take a long integer IP argument in its constructor, or process a string with the dotted-quad representation of an IP address using its Parse() method. The Dns class also provides a mechanism to look up, or *resolve*, names to IP addresses (e.g., *server.example.com*). Since in the modern Internet it is not uncommon for a single server to resolve to multiple

IP addresses or name aliases, the results are returned in a *container class* IPHostEntry, which contains an array of one or more string host names and IPAddress class instances.

The Dns class has several methods for resolving IP addresses. The GetHostName() method takes no arguments and returns a string containing the local host name. The GetHostByName() and Resolve() methods are basically identical; they take a string argument containing the host name to be looked up and returns the IP address and host name information for the supplied input in the form of an IPHostEntry class instance. The Get-HostByAddress() method takes a string argument containing the dotted-quad string representation of an IP address and also returns host information in an IPHostEntry instance.

Our first program example, IPAddressExample.cs, demonstrates the use of the Dns, IPAddress, and IPHostEntry classes. The program takes a list of names or IP addresses as command-line parameters and prints the name and an IP address of the local host, followed by the names and IP addresses of the hosts specified on the command line.

IPAddressExample.cs

```
0   using System;              // For String and Console
1   using System.Net;          // For Dns, IPHostEntry, IPAddress
2   using System.Net.Sockets;  // For SocketException
3
4   class IPAddressExample {
5
6     static void PrintHostInfo(String host) {
7
8       try {
9         IPHostEntry hostInfo;
10
11        // Attempt to resolve DNS for given host or address
12        hostInfo = Dns.Resolve(host);
13
14        // Display the primary host name
15        Console.WriteLine("\tCanonical Name: " + hostInfo.HostName);
16
17        // Display list of IP addresses for this host
18        Console.Write("\tIP Addresses:   ");
19        foreach (IPAddress ipaddr in hostInfo.AddressList) {
20          Console.Write(ipaddr.ToString() + " ");
21        }
22        Console.WriteLine();
23
24        // Display list of alias names for this host
25        Console.Write("\tAliases:        ");
26        foreach (String alias in hostInfo.Aliases) {
```

```
27          Console.Write(alias + " ");
28        }
29        Console.WriteLine("\n");
30      } catch (Exception) {
31        Console.WriteLine("\tUnable to resolve host: " + host + "\n");
32      }
33    }
34
35    static void Main(string[] args) {
36
37      // Get and print local host info
38      try {
39        Console.WriteLine("Local Host:");
40        String localHostName = Dns.GetHostName();
41        Console.WriteLine("\tHost Name:      " + localHostName);
42
43        PrintHostInfo(localHostName);
44      } catch (Exception) {
45        Console.WriteLine("Unable to resolve local host\n");
46      }
47
48      // Get and print info for hosts given on command line
49      foreach (String arg in args) {
50        Console.WriteLine(arg + ":");
51        PrintHostInfo(arg);
52      }
53    }
54  }
```

IPAddressExample.cs

1. PrintHostInfo()**: look up host/address/alias info for the host name argument and print it to the console:** lines 6–33

   ■ **Retrieve an** IPHostEntry **class instance for the specified host:** lines 11–12
   Call Dns.Resolve() with the host name argument. If successful, hostInfo will reference an IPHostEntry class instance containing information for the specified host. If the lookup fails, code execution will drop to the catch block on lines 30–32.

   ■ **Print the canonical name:** lines 14–15
   DNS allows a host name to have one "canonical" or true name and zero or more aliases. The canonical name is populated in the HostName property of the IPHostEntry.

∎ **Display the list of IP address(es):** lines 17–22
Loop through all the IP address(es) contained in the AddressList property, which is an array of IPAddress class instances.

∎ **Display the list of alias host names:** lines 24–29
Loop through any host name aliases contained in the Aliases property, which is an array of Strings. If a host name being looked up does not have any aliases, this array will be empty.

2. **Print information about the local host:** lines 37–46

∎ **Get and print the local host name using** Dns.GetHostName(): lines 37–41
Note that the GetHostName() method will only return the host name, not the fully-qualified Internet DNS name.

∎ **Call** PrintHostInfo() **with the host name to retrieve and print all local host info:** line 43

∎ **Catch any exceptions getting the local host name:** lines 44–46

3. **Loop through all command-line arguments and call** PrintHostInfo() **for each of them:** lines 48–52

To use this application to find information about the local host and our publisher's Web server (*www.mkp.com*), do the following:

```
C:\> IPAddressExample www.mkp.com
```

```
Local Host:
        Host Name:       tractor
        Canonical Name:  tractor.farm.com
        IP Addresses:    169.1.1.2
        Aliases:
```

```
www.mkp.com:
        Canonical Name:  www.mkp.com
        IP Addresses:    129.35.78.178
        Aliases:
```

If we know the IP address of a host (e.g., 169.1.1.1), we find the name of the host by

```
C:\> IPAddressExample 169.1.1.1
```

```
Local Host:
        Host Name:       tractor
        Canonical Name:  tractor.farm.com
        IP Addresses:    169.1.1.2
        Aliases:
```

```
169.1.1.1:
        Canonical Name:  base.farm.com
        IP Addresses:    169.1.1.1
        Aliases:         gateway.farm.com
```

When the name service is not available for some reason—say, the program is running on a machine that is not connected to any network—attempting to identify a host by name may fail. Moreover, it may take a significant amount of time to do so, as the system tries various ways to resolve the name to an IP address.[1] It is therefore good to know that you can always refer to a host using the IP address in dotted-quad notation. In any of our examples, if a remote host is specified by name, the host running the example must be configured to convert names to addresses, or the example won't work. If you can ping a host using one of its names (e.g., run the command "ping *server.example.com*"), then the examples should work with names. If your ping test fails or the example hangs, try specifying the host by IP address, which avoids the name-to-address conversion altogether.

IPAddress Summary[2]

Description

The IPAddress class contains the address of an interface on an IP network.

Selected Constructor

public IPAddress(**long** *address*);
Returns an IPAddress instance with the value of the supplied **long** argument.

Selected Methods

public override bool Equals(**object** *comparand*);
Compare two IPAddress instances and return **true** if they contain the same IP address.

public static short HostToNetworkOrder(**short**);

public static int HostToNetworkOrder(**int**);

public static long HostToNetworkOrder(**long**);

public static short NetworkToHostOrder(**short**);

public static int NetworkToHostOrder(**int**);

---

[1] In Chapter 4 we discuss how asynchronous operations may be performed, which is also applicable to Dns lookups.

[2] For each .NET networking class described in this text, we present only a summary of the primary methods and properties and omit those whose use is beyond the scope of this text. As with everything in .NET, the specification is a moving target. This information is included to provide an overall picture of the .NET socket interface, not as a final authority. We encourage the reader to refer to the API specification from *www.msdn.microsoft.com* as the current and definitive source.

public static long NetworkToHostOrder(**long**);
Host-to-network and network-to-host ordering conversion methods (see Section 3.1.2).

public static IPAddress Parse(**string** *address*);
Convert a string in dotted quad notation to an IPAddress instance. Throws ArgumentNullException, FormatException.

public override string ToString();
Returns the string dotted quad notation for the IPAddress instance.

Selected Fields

public static readonly IPAddress Any;
Contains a value of 0.0.0.0, any network interface.

public static readonly IPAddress Broadcast;
Contains a value of 255.255.255.255, all hosts on a subnet.

public static readonly IPAddress Loopback;
Contains a value of 127.0.0.1, loopback for the local host.

IPHostEntry Summary

Description

IPHostEntry is a container class returned by Dns class methods GetHostByName(), GetHostByAddress() and Resolve(). The class contains Domain Name System (DNS) information about a host, including host name, array of IP addresses, and array of alias host names.

Selected Properties

public IPAddress[] AddressList {get; set;}
An array of IPAddress instances.

public string[] Aliases {get; set;}
An array of strings containing DNS alias host names.

public string HostName {get; set;}
A string containing the primary canonical host name.

Dns Summary

Description

The Dns class provides a number of static methods to retrieve information about a host name or IP address from the Domain Name System (DNS).

Selected Methods

public static IPHostEntry GetHostByAddress(**IPAddress** *address*);
Attempts to reverse lookup an IPAddress instance and provide an IPHostEntry containing the host's DNS information. Throws ArgumentNullException, Socket-Exception, SecurityException.

public static IPHostEntry GetHostByAddress(**string** *address*);
Attempts to reverse lookup a string IP address in dotted-quad notation and provide an IPHostEntry instance containing the host's DNS information. Throws ArgumentNullException, SocketException, FormatException, SecurityException.

public static IPHostEntry GetHostByName(**string** *hostname*);
Does a DNS lookup on the string host name argument and provides an IPHostEntry instance containing the host's DNS information. Throws ArgumentNullException, SocketException, SecurityException.

public static string GetHostName();
Returns a string containing the host name of the local computer.

public static IPHostEntry Resolve(**string** *hostname*);
Does a DNS lookup on the string host name argument and provides an IPHostEntry instance containing the host's DNS information. Throws ArgumentNullException, SocketException, SecurityException.

2.2 Socket Implementation in .NET

Before we begin describing the details of the .NET socket classes, it is useful to give a brief overview and history of sockets on Microsoft Windows. Sockets was initially created for the Berkeley Software Distribution (BSD) of UNIX. A version of sockets for Microsoft Windows called WinSock 1.1 was initially released in 1992 and is currently on version 2.0. With some minor differences, WinSock provides the standard sockets functions available in the Berkeley sockets C interface (the C version of this book describes that interface in detail [24]).

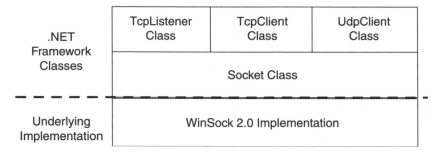

Figure 2.1: Relationship of Socket classes.

In 2002 Microsoft released the standardized API framework known as .NET, which provides a unified class library across all of the programming languages Microsoft offers. Among the features of the library are higher level classes that hide much of the implementation detail and simplify many programming tasks. However, abstraction can sometimes hide some of the flexibility and power of a lower level interface. In order to allow access to the underlying sockets interface, Microsoft implemented a .NET Socket class, which is a wrapper around the WinSock socket functions and has most of the versatility (and complexity) of sockets interface exposed. Then three higher-level socket classes, TcpClient, TcpListener, and UdpClient, were implemented by using the .NET Socket wrapper class. In fact, these classes have a protected property that is an instance of the Socket class they are using. Pictorially this can be represented as shown in Figure 2.1.

Why is this important to know? First, to clarify what we mean when we refer to a "socket." The word *socket* has come to mean many different things in network programming, from an API to a class name or instance. In general when we refer to an uppercase "Socket" we mean the .NET class, while a lowercase "socket" refers to a socket instance using any of the .NET socket classes.

Second, the underlying implementation occasionally becomes apparent to the .NET programmer. Sometimes the Socket class needs to be utilized to take advantage of advanced functionality. Some components of the underlying WinSock implementation are also still visible, such as the use of WinSock error codes, which are available via the ErrorCode property of SocketException and can be used to determine exactly what type of error has occurred. The WinSock error codes are discussed in more detail in the Appendix.

2.3 TCP Sockets

The .NET framework provides two classes specifically for TCP: TcpClient and TcpListener. These classes provide a higher level abstraction of the Socket class, but as we will see there are instances when advanced functionality is available only through direct use of the Socket class.

An instance of any of these classes represents one end of a TCP connection. A *TCP connection* is an abstract two-way channel whose ends are each identified by an IP address and port number. As we will see, .NET uses the EndPoint class and its subclass IPEnd-Point to abstract this concept. Before being used for communication, a TCP connection must go through a setup phase, which starts with the client's TCP sending a connection request to the server's TCP. An instance of TcpListener listens for TCP connection requests and creates a new socket (in the form of a TcpClient or Socket instance) to handle each incoming connection.

2.3.1   TCP Client

A TCP client initiates communication with a server that is passively waiting to be contacted. The typical TCP client goes through three steps:

1. **Construct an instance of** TcpClient: a TCP connection can be created implicitly in the constructor by specifying the remote host and port, or explicitly using the Connect() method.

2. **Communicate using the socket's stream:** A connected instance of TcpClient contains a NetworkStream that can be used like any other .NET I/O stream.

3. **Close the connection:** Call the Close() method of TcpClient.

Our first TCP application, called TcpEchoClient.cs, is a client that communicates with an *echo server* using TCP. An echo server simply repeats whatever it receives back to the client. The string to be echoed is provided as a command-line argument to our client. Many systems include an echo server for debugging and testing purposes. To test if the standard echo server is running, try telnetting to port 7 (the default echo port) on the server (e.g., at command line "telnet server.example.com 7" or use your telnet application of choice). If not, you can run this client against the TcpEchoServer.cs server from the next section.

TcpEchoClient.cs

```
0   using System;              // For String, Int32, Console, ArgumentException
1   using System.Text;         // For Encoding
2   using System.IO;           // For IOException
3   using System.Net.Sockets;  // For TcpClient, NetworkStream, SocketException
4
5   class TcpEchoClient {
6
```

```
7    static void Main(string[] args) {
8
9      if ((args.Length < 2) || (args.Length > 3)) { // Test for correct # of args
10       throw new ArgumentException("Parameters: <Server> <Word> [<Port>]");
11     }
12
13     String server = args[0];   // Server name or IP address
14
15     // Convert input String to bytes
16     byte[] byteBuffer = Encoding.ASCII.GetBytes(args[1]);
17
18     // Use port argument if supplied, otherwise default to 7
19     int servPort = (args.Length == 3) ? Int32.Parse(args[2]) : 7;
20
21     TcpClient client = null;
22     NetworkStream netStream = null;
23
24     try {
25       // Create socket that is connected to server on specified port
26       client = new TcpClient(server, servPort);
27
28       Console.WriteLine("Connected to server... sending echo string");
29
30       netStream = client.GetStream();
31
32       // Send the encoded string to the server
33       netStream.Write(byteBuffer, 0, byteBuffer.Length);
34
35       Console.WriteLine("Sent {0} bytes to server...", byteBuffer.Length);
36
37       int totalBytesRcvd = 0;   // Total bytes received so far
38       int bytesRcvd = 0;        // Bytes received in last read
39
40       // Receive the same string back from the server
41       while (totalBytesRcvd < byteBuffer.Length) {
42         if ((bytesRcvd = netStream.Read(byteBuffer, totalBytesRcvd,
43             byteBuffer.Length - totalBytesRcvd)) == 0) {
44           Console.WriteLine("Connection closed prematurely.");
45           break;
46         }
47         totalBytesRcvd += bytesRcvd;
48       }
49
```

```
50        Console.WriteLine("Received {0} bytes from server: {1}", totalBytesRcvd,
51                          Encoding.ASCII.GetString(byteBuffer, 0, totalBytesRcvd));
52
53      } catch (Exception e) {
54        Console.WriteLine(e.Message);
55      } finally {
56        netStream.Close();
57        client.Close();
58      }
59    }
60  }
```

TcpEchoClient.cs

1. **Application setup and parameter parsing:** lines 9–22

   ■ **Convert the echo string:** lines 15–16
   TCP sockets send and receive sequences of bytes. The static method Encoding.ASCII.GetBytes() returns a byte array representation of the string argument using the ASCII character set. .NET also provides encoding classes for Unicode as well as other character sets.

   ■ **Determine the port of the echo server:** line 19
   The default echo port is 7. We can specify the port with an optional third parameter, which is converted from a string to an integer with Int32.Parse().

2. **TCP socket creation:** lines 25–28
   The TcpClient constructor creates the socket and implicitly establishes a connection to the specified server, identified by either name or IP address and a port number. Note that the underlying TCP deals only with IP addresses. If a name is given, the implementation uses DNS to resolve it to the corresponding address. If any error occurs accessing the socket, the constructor throws a SocketException.

3. **Get socket stream:** line 30
   Associated with each connected TcpClient socket instance is a NetworkStream, which is a subclass of Stream. The stream classes provide an abstraction for a generic view of a sequence of bytes. We send data over the socket by writing bytes to the NetworkStream just as we would any other stream, and we receive by reading bytes from the NetworkStream.

4. **Send the string to the echo server:** lines 32–33
   The Write() method of NetworkStream transmits the given byte array over the connection to the server. The arguments to Write() are (1) the byte buffer containing the data to be sent, (2) the byte offset into the buffer where the data to be sent starts, and (3) a total number of bytes to send.

5. **Receive the reply from the echo server:** lines 40–48
   Since we know the number of bytes to expect from the echo server, we can repeatedly receive bytes until we have received the same number of bytes we sent. This particular form of Read() takes three parameters: (1) buffer to receive to, (2) byte offset into the buffer where the first byte received should be placed, and (3) the maximum number of bytes to be placed in the buffer. Read() blocks until some data is available, reads up to the specified number of bytes, then returns the number of bytes actually placed in the buffer (which may be less than the given maximum). The loop simply fills up *byteBuffer* until we receive as many bytes as we sent. If the TCP connection is closed by the other end, Read() returns 0. For the client, this indicates that the server prematurely closed the socket.

   Why not just a single read? TCP does not preserve Read() and Write() message boundaries. That is, even though we sent the echo string with a single Write(), the echo server may receive it in multiple chunks. Even if the echo string is handled in one chunk by the echo server, the reply may still be broken into pieces by TCP. One of the most common errors for beginners is the assumption that data sent by a single Write() will always be received by a single Read().

6. **Print echoed string:** lines 50–51
   To print the server's response, we must convert the byte array to a string using the static Encoding.ASCII.GetString() method.

7. **Error handling:** lines 53–54
   Several types of exception could be thrown in this try block, including Socket-Exception for the TcpClient constructor and IOException for the NetworkStream Write() and Read() methods. By using the base Exception class, from which all other exception classes are derived from, we catch whatever is thrown and print an indication.

8. **Close stream and socket:** lines 55–58
   The finally block of the try/catch will always be executed. Whether an error occurred and was caught or the client has successfully finished receiving all of the echoed data, the finally block is executed and closes the NetworkStream and TcpClient.

   We can communicate with an echo server named *server.example.com* with IP address 169.1.1.1 in either of the following ways:

```
C:\> TcpEchoClient server.example.com "Echo this!"
Connected to server... sending echo string
Sent 10 bytes to server...
Received 10 bytes from server: Echo this!

C:\> TcpEchoClient 169.1.1.1 "Echo this again!"
Connected to server... sending echo string
Sent 16 bytes to server...
Received 16 bytes from server: Echo this again!
```

The above example assumes that either a default echo server or the TcpEchoServer program from the next section is running to respond to the request. The running of the TcpEchoServer program for the above requests would look like:

```
C:\> TcpEchoServer
Handling client - echoed 10 bytes.
Handling client - echoed 16 bytes.
^C
C:\>
```

See TcpEchoClientGUI.cs on this book's website (www.mkp.com/practical/csharpsockets) for an implementation of the TCP echo client with a graphical interface.

TcpClient Summary

Description

TcpClient provides simple methods for connecting to, sending, and receiving data over a TCP connection. The TcpClient method GetStream() provides access to a NetworkStream to abstract the sending and receiving of data.

Constructors

public TcpClient();

public TcpClient(**IPEndPoint** *localEP*);

public TcpClient(**string** *hostname*, **int** *port*);
Creates a new instance of the TcpClient class. The TcpClient constructors have optional arguments for a local interface to bind to (IPEndPoint), or the server to connect to (string hostname/IP and integer port). If the server is not specified, you must call Connect() before sending data. If the server is specified, the connect is done implicitly. Throws ArgumentNullException, ArgumentOutOfRangeException, SocketException.

Selected Methods

public void Close();
Closes the TCP connection. Note that when using a NetworkStream it is preferable to close the NetworkStream that will implicitly close the underlying socket. Closing a TcpClient does not free the resources of its NetworkStream.

public void Connect(**IPEndPoint**);

public void Connect(**IPAddress** *address*, **int** *port*);

public void Connect(**string** *host name*, **int** *port*);
Connects to a remote host using the specified destination parameters. Throws
ArgumentNullException, ArgumentOutOfRangeException, SocketException, Object
DisposedException.

public NetworkStream GetStream();
Returns a NetworkStream instance used to send and receive data. Throws Invalid-
OperationException, ObjectDisposedException.

Selected Properties

protected Socket Client {get; set;}
Gets or sets the underlying Socket. Since Client is a protected property, it may only
be accessed by classes that extend TcpClient. This is useful for accessing socket
options that are not directly accessible from the TcpClient API directly.

EndPoint

Description

EndPoint is an abstract base class that represents a network connection point. The
IPEndPoint class derives from this class.

Constructor

protected EndPoint();
This constructor is called by derived class constructors.

Selected Methods

public virtual string ToString();
Returns a string representation of the current EndPoint.

IPEndPoint

Description

IPEndPoint represents a TCP/IP network endpoint as an IP address and a port number.

Constructor

> **public** IPEndPoint(**long** *address*, **int** *port*);

> **public** IPEndPoint(**IPAddress** *address*, **int** *port*);
> The constructor initializes a new instance of the IPEndPoint class with the specified IP address (in either **long** or IPAddress form) and integer port number.

Selected Methods

> **public virtual string** ToString();
> Returns a string representation of the current IPEndPoint.

Selected Properties

> **public IPAddress** Address {get; set;}
> An IPAddress instance containing the IP address of the endpoint.

> **public int** Port {get; set;}
> An integer value representing the TCP or UDP port number of the endpoint. The port must be in the range **MinPort** to **MaxPort**.

2.3.2 TCP Server

We now turn our attention to constructing a server. The server's job is to set up an endpoint for clients to connect to and passively wait for connections. The typical TCP server goes through two steps:

1. Construct a TcpListener instance, specifying the local address and port, and call the Start() method. This socket listens for incoming connections on the specified port.

2. Repeatedly:
   - Call the AcceptTcpClient() method of TcpListener to get the next incoming client connection. Upon establishment of a new client connection, an instance of TcpClient for the new connection is created and returned by the AcceptTcp-Client() call.
   - Communicate with the client using the Read() and Write() methods of TcpClient's NetworkStream.
   - Close the new client socket connection and stream using the Close() methods of NetworkStream and TcpClient.

   Note that in C#, the TcpClient class is used to access a TCP connection, whether in the client or the server. The same class can be used because the TCP protocol really makes no distinction between client and server, especially once the connection is established.

As an alternative to AcceptTcpClient(), the TcpListener class also has an Accept-Socket() method that returns a Socket instance for the incoming client connection. The Socket class is described in more detail later in Section 2.5.

Our next example, TcpEchoServer.cs, implements the echo service used by our client program. The server is very simple. It runs forever, repeatedly accepting a connection, receiving and echoing bytes until the connection is closed by the client, and then closing the client socket.

TcpEchoServer.cs

```
0   using System;              // For Console, Int32, ArgumentException, Environment
1   using System.Net;          // For IPAddress
2   using System.Net.Sockets;  // For TcpListener, TcpClient
3
4   class TcpEchoServer {
5
6     private const int BUFSIZE = 32; // Size of receive buffer
7
8     static void Main(string[] args) {
9
10      if (args.Length > 1) // Test for correct # of args
11        throw new ArgumentException("Parameters: [<Port>]");
12
13      int servPort = (args.Length == 1) ? Int32.Parse(args[0]): 7;
14
15      TcpListener listener = null;
16
17      try {
18        // Create a TCPListener to accept client connections
19        listener = new TcpListener(IPAddress.Any, servPort);
20        listener.Start();
21      } catch (SocketException se) {
22        Console.WriteLine(se.ErrorCode + ": " + se.Message);
23        Environment.Exit(se.ErrorCode);
24      }
25
26      byte[] rcvBuffer = new byte[BUFSIZE]; // Receive buffer
27      int bytesRcvd;                        // Received byte count
28
29      for (;;) { // Run forever, accepting and servicing connections
30
31        TcpClient client = null;
32        NetworkStream netStream = null;
```

```
33
34        try {
35          client = listener.AcceptTcpClient(); // Get client connection
36          netStream = client.GetStream();
37          Console.Write("Handling client - ");
38
39          // Receive until client closes connection, indicated by 0 return value
40          int totalBytesEchoed = 0;
41          while ((bytesRcvd = netStream.Read(rcvBuffer, 0, rcvBuffer.Length)) > 0) {
42            netStream.Write(rcvBuffer, 0, bytesRcvd);
43            totalBytesEchoed += bytesRcvd;
44          }
45          Console.WriteLine("echoed {0} bytes.", totalBytesEchoed);
46
47          // Close the stream and socket. We are done with this client!
48          netStream.Close();
49          client.Close();
50
51        } catch (Exception e) {
52          Console.WriteLine(e.Message);
53          netStream.Close();
54        }
55      }
56    }
57 }
```

TcpEchoServer.cs

1. **Application setup and parameter parsing:** lines 10–15

2. **Server socket creation:** lines 17–24
   listener is initialized with IPAddress.Any and the specified server port number. IPAddress.Any is 0.0.0.0 and indicates that the *listener* will listen on any available local interface (if you are running on a machine that is multihomed, this field can be used to specify the interface to listen on). The TcpListener listens for client connection requests on the port specified in the constructor. Be careful to use a port that is not in use by another application, or a SocketException will be thrown (see Chapter 5 for more details). The Start() method initiates the underlying socket, binds it to the local endpoint, and begins listening for incoming connection attempts.

3. **Loop forever, iteratively handling incoming connections:** lines 29–53

   ■ **Accept an incoming connection:** line 35
   The sole purpose of a TcpListener instance is to supply a new, connected TcpClient instance for each new TCP connection. When the server is ready to

handle a client, it calls AcceptTcpClient(), which blocks until an incoming connection is made to the TcpListener's port. AcceptTcpClient() then returns an instance of TcpClient that is already *connected* to the remote socket and ready for reading and writing (we also could have used the AcceptSocket() method instead).

▪ **Get** NetworkStream: line 36
The TcpClient method GetStream() returns an instance of a NetworkStream, which is used for reading and writing to its socket.

▪ **Receive and repeat data until the client closes:** lines 39–45
The while loop repeatedly reads bytes from the NetworkStream and immediately writes them back to the stream until the client closes the connection, which is indicated by a return value of 0 from Read(). The Read() method takes a byte array, an offset at which to begin placing bytes, and an integer indicating the maximum number of bytes to be placed in the array. It blocks until data is available and returns the number of bytes actually placed in the array (which may be less than the specified maximum). If the other end closes the connection before any bytes have been received, Read() returns 0.

The Write() method of NetworkStream similarly takes three parameters and transmits the specified number of bytes from the given array, beginning at the specified offset (in this case, 0). There is another form of Write() that only takes a byte array argument and transmits *all* the bytes contained therein to the other end of the TCP connection; if we had used that form, we might have transmited bytes that were not received from the client!

Any parameter inconsistencies (e.g., offset or length greater than the actual length of the bytes array) result in an exception being thrown.

▪ **Close the client stream and socket:** lines 48–49
Close the NetworkStream and the TcpClient socket.

▪ **Exception handling:** lines 51–54
A server should be robust enough to handle a malfunctioning or malicious client without crashing. Any exception that occurs during processing is caught here and written to the console. The NetworkStream and its underlying socket are closed to clean up. Note that this catch block is within the for loop, so after handling the exception the loop continues and another client can be serviced.

TcpListener Summary

Description

TcpListener listens for connections from TCP network clients. The constructor takes the local interface and optionally the local port to listen on. The Start() method begins listening for incoming connection requests. The AcceptTcpClient() and AcceptSocket() methods accept incoming connections and return a TcpClient or Socket instance, respectively, that is already connected to the remote client and ready for sending and receiving. The Stop() method stops listening for connections and closes the TcpListener.

Constructors

public TcpListener(**int** *port*);
(obsoleted in 1.1 .NET SDK)

public TcpListener(**IPEndPoint** *localEP*);

public TcpListener(**IPAddress** *address*, **int** *port*);
The constructor has three forms: port only, IPEndPoint instance, or IPAddress and port. When an address is specified it represents the local interface to listen on. Note that starting in .NET 1.1, the local interface is required and the port-only constructor is deprecated. Throws ArgumentNullException, ArgumentOutOfRangeException.

Selected Methods

public Socket AcceptSocket();
Accepts a pending connection request and returns a Socket used to send and receive data. Throws InvalidOperationException.

public TcpClient AcceptTcpClient();
Accepts a pending connection request and returns a TcpClient used to send and receive data. Throws InvalidOperationException.

public bool Pending();
Returns **true** if there are pending incoming connections that can be accepted. Throws InvalidOperationException.

public void Start();
Start initializes the underlying socket, binds it, and begins listening for network requests. Throws SocketException.

public void Stop();
Stops listening for incoming connections and closes the TcpListener. Any accepted TcpClient or Socket instances should be closed separately. Throws SocketException.

Selected Properties

public EndPoint LocalEndpoint {get;}
Gets the underlying local bound EndPoint.

protected Socket Server {get;}
Gets the underlying network Socket. Since this is a protected property, it can only be accessed by classes that extend TcpListener. This is useful for accessing socket options that are not directly accessible from the TcpListener API.

2.3.3 Streams

As illustrated by the preceding examples, the primary paradigm for I/O in the .NET framework is the *stream* abstraction. A stream is simply an ordered sequence of bytes. .NET *streams* support both reading and writing bytes to a stream. In our TCP client and server, each TcpClient or TcpListener instance holds a NetworkStream instance. When we write to the stream of a TcpClient, the bytes can (eventually) be read from the stream of the TcpListener at the other end of the connection. The Socket and UdpClient classes use byte arrays instead of streams to send and receive data. If there is an error reading or writing, a NetworkStream will throw an IOException. See Section 3.2 for more details on streams.

NetworkStream

Description

NetworkStream is a subclass of Stream, and provides the underlying stream of data for network I/O.

Selected Methods

public virtual void Close();
The Close() method closes the NetworkStream and closes the underlying socket if it owns it.

public abstract int Read(**byte[]** *buffer*, **int** *offset*, **int** *length*);
The Read() method reads data from the network stream into the byte buffer argument. The offset within the buffer and number of bytes to read are also specified. Read() returns the number of bytes read. Throws ArgumentNullException, Argument-Exception, IOException.

public abstract void Write(**byte[]** *buffer*, **int** *offset*, **int** *length*);
The Write() method sends the contents of a supplied byte buffer argument to the network. An offset within the byte buffer and number of bytes to write are also supplied as arguments. Throws ArgumentNullException, ArgumentException, IOException.

Selected Properties

public virtual bool DataAvailable { get; }
Returns true if data is available to read on the stream, false if there is no data available to read.

2.4 UDP Sockets

UDP provides an end-to-end service different from that of TCP. In fact, UDP performs only two functions: (1) it adds another layer of addressing (ports) to that of IP, and (2) it detects data corruption that may occur in transit and discards any corrupted messages. Because of this simplicity, UDP sockets have some characteristics that are different from the TCP sockets we saw earlier. For example, UDP sockets do not have to be connected before being used. Where TCP is analogous to telephone communication, UDP is analogous to communicating by mail: You do not have to "connect" before you send the package or letter, but you do have to specify the destination address for each one. Similarly, each message—called a *datagram*—carries its own address information and is independent of all others. In receiving, a UDP socket is like a mailbox into which letters or packages from many different sources can be placed. As soon as it is created, a UDP socket can be used to send/receive messages to/from any address and to/from many different addresses in succession.

Another difference between UDP sockets and TCP sockets is the way in which they deal with message boundaries: *UDP sockets preserve them.* This makes receiving an application message simpler, in some ways, than it is with TCP sockets (this is discussed further in Section 2.4.3). A final difference is that the end-to-end transport service UDP provides its best effort: There is no guarantee that a message sent via a UDP socket will arrive at its destination, and messages can be delivered in a different order than they were sent (just like letters sent through the mail). A program using UDP sockets must therefore be prepared to deal with loss and reordering. (We'll provide an example of this in Section 2.5.4.)

Given this additional burden, why would an application use UDP instead of TCP? One reason is efficiency. If the application exchanges only a small amount of data—say, a single request message from client to server and a single response message in the other direction—TCP's connection establishment phase at least doubles the number of messages (and the number of round-trip delays) required for the communication. Another reason is flexibility. When something other than a reliable byte-stream service is required, UDP provides a minimal overhead platform on which to implement whatever is needed.

The .NET framework provides UDP sockets functionality using the class UdpClient, or Socket for more advanced options. The UdpClient class allows for both sending and receiving of UDP packets, and can be used to construct both a UDP client and server.

2.4.1 UDP Client

A UDP client begins by sending a datagram to a server that is passively waiting to be contacted. The typical UDP client goes through three steps:

1. Construct an instance of UdpClient, optionally specifying the local address and port.

2. Communicate by sending and receiving datagrams (byte arrays) using the Send() and Receive() methods of UdpClient.

3. When finished, deallocate the socket using the Close() method of UdpClient.

Unlike a TcpClient, a UdpClient does not have to be constructed (or connected) with a specific destination address. This illustrates one of the major differences between TCP and UDP. A TCP socket is required to establish a connection with another TCP socket on a specified host and port before any data can be exchanged, and, thereafter, it *only* communicates with that socket until it is closed. A UDP socket, on the other hand, is not required to establish a connection before communication, and each datagram can be sent and received from a different destination. The Connect() method of UdpClient does allow the specification of the remote address and port, but its use is optional. Unlike the TCP version of Connect(), the UDP version merely sets the default destination and does not actually cause any connection-setup messages to be transmitted through the network.

Our UDP echo client, UdpEchoClient.cs, sends a datagram containing the string to be echoed and prints whatever it receives back from the server. A UDP echo server simply repeats each datagram that it receives back to the client. Of course, a UDP client only communicates with a UDP server. Many systems include a UDP echo server for debugging and testing purposes, or you can run the UDP echo server example from the next section.

UdpEchoClient.cs

```
0   using System;              // For String, Int32, Console
1   using System.Text;         // For Encoding
2   using System.Net;          // For IPEndPoint
3   using System.Net.Sockets;  // For UdpClient, SocketException
4
5   class UdpEchoClient {
6
7     static void Main(string[] args) {
8
9       if ((args.Length < 2) || (args.Length > 3)) { // Test for correct # of args
10        throw new System.ArgumentException("Parameters: <Server> <Word> [<Port>]");
11      }
12
13      String server = args[0];     // Server name or IP address
14
15      // Use port argument if supplied, otherwise default to 7
16      int servPort = (args.Length == 3) ? Int32.Parse(args[2]) : 7;
17
18      // Convert input String to an array of bytes
19      byte[] sendPacket = Encoding.ASCII.GetBytes(args[1]);
20
21      // Create a UdpClient instance
22      UdpClient client = new UdpClient();
23
```

```
24      try {
25        // Send the echo string to the specified host and port
26        client.Send(sendPacket, sendPacket.Length, server, servPort);
27
28        Console.WriteLine("Sent {0} bytes to the server...", sendPacket.Length);
29
30        // This IPEndPoint instance will be populated with the remote sender's
31        // endpoint information after the Receive() call
32        IPEndPoint remoteIPEndPoint = new IPEndPoint(IPAddress.Any, 0);
33
34        // Attempt echo reply receive
35        byte[] rcvPacket = client.Receive(ref remoteIPEndPoint);
36
37        Console.WriteLine("Received {0} bytes from {1}: {2}",
38                          rcvPacket.Length, remoteIPEndPoint,
39                          Encoding.ASCII.GetString(rcvPacket, 0, rcvPacket.Length));
40      } catch (SocketException se) {
41        Console.WriteLine(se.ErrorCode + ": " + se.Message);
42      }
43
44      client.Close();
45    }
46  }
```

UdpEchoClient.cs

1. **Application setup and parameter parsing:** lines 9–19
   - **Convert argument to bytes:** lines 17–19

2. **UDP socket creation:** lines 21–22
   This instance of UdpClient can send datagrams to any UDP socket. The destination host and port can be set in the constructor, in the Connect() call, or directly in the Send() call. In this case we set it in the Send() call. If we specify a host name, it is converted to an IP address for us.

3. **Send the datagram and receive the response:** lines 24–42
   - **Send the datagram:** lines 25–26
   The Send() call takes the datagram byte array and the number of bytes to send as arguments. Send() can also take optional arguments specifying the destination address and port (either as a string host name/IP and integer port, or as an IPEndPoint instance). If the destination arguments are omitted, they must have been specified in either the UdpClient constructor or the Connect() call. If you do not include the destination arguments in the constructor or Connect(), you can

make subsequent calls to Send() with different destinations. However, if you do specify destination arguments in the constructor or Connect(), you cannot override the destination in the Send(), and attempting to do so will generate an InvalidOperationException.

- **Create a remote IP end point for receiving:** lines 30–32
  The IPEndPoint class specifies an address and port combination. This IPEndPoint instance will be passed as a reference to the Receive() method, which will populate it with the remote sender's IP address and port information.

- **Handle datagram reception:** lines 34–35
  Receive() blocks until it receives a datagram. When it returns, the *remoteIPEndPoint* instance will contain the address and port information for the remote host that sent the packet just received.

4. **Print reception results:** lines 37–39

5. **Close the socket:** line 44

We invoke the UDP client using the same parameters as used in the TCP client:

```
C:\> UdpEchoClient 169.1.1.2 "Echo this!"
Sent 10 bytes to the server...
Received 10 bytes from 169.1.1.2: Echo this!
```

One consequence of using UDP is that datagrams can be lost. In the case of our echo protocol, either the echo request from the client or the echo reply from the server may be lost in the network. Recall that our TCP echo client sends an echo string and then blocks with a Read() waiting for a reply. If we try the same strategy with our UDP echo client and the echo request datagram is lost, our client will block forever on Receive(). To avoid this problem, our client can implement a timeout on the blocking Receive() call. In Section 2.5.4 we introduce UdpEchoClientTimeoutSocket.cs, which modifies UdpEchoClient.cs to do just that.

2.4.2   UDP Server

Like a TCP server, a UDP server's job is to set up a communication endpoint and passively wait for the client to initiate the communication; however, since UDP is connectionless, UDP communication is initiated by a datagram from the client, without going through a connection setup as in TCP. This means receiving a datagram as a server is really no different from receiving a datagram as a client. As a result, instead of separate classes for a UDP client and server, the UdpClient class is used to implement the server as well as the client.

The typical UDP server goes through four steps:

1. Construct an instance of UdpClient, specifying the local port. The server is now ready to receive datagrams from any client.

2. Receive a packet using the `Receive()` method of `UdpClient`. The `Receive()` method takes a reference to an `IPEndPoint` instance as an argument, and when the call returns the `IPEndPoint` contains the client's address so we know where to send the reply.

3. Communicate by sending and receiving datagram packets using the `Send()` and `Receive()` methods of `UdpClient`.

4. When finished, deallocate the socket using the `Close()` method of `UdpClient`.

Our next program example, `UdpEchoServer.cs`, implements the UDP version of the echo server. The server is very simple: it loops forever, receiving datagrams and then sending the same datagrams back to the client.

UdpEchoServer.cs

```
0   using System;           // For Console, Int32, ArgumentException, Environment
1   using System.Net;       // For IPEndPoint
2   using System.Net.Sockets; // For UdpClient, SocketException
3
4   class UdpEchoServer {
5
6     static void Main(string[] args) {
7
8       if (args.Length > 1) { // Test for correct # of args
9         throw new ArgumentException("Parameters: <Port>");
10      }
11
12      int servPort = (args.Length == 1) ? Int32.Parse(args[0]) : 7;
13
14      UdpClient client = null;
15
16      try {
17        // Create an instance of UdpClient on the port to listen on
18        client = new UdpClient(servPort);
19      } catch (SocketException se) {
20        Console.WriteLine(se.ErrorCode + ": " + se.Message);
21        Environment.Exit(se.ErrorCode);
22      }
23
24      // Create an IPEndPoint instance that will be passed as a reference
25      // to the Receive() call and be populated with the remote client info
26      IPEndPoint remoteIPEndPoint = new IPEndPoint(IPAddress.Any, 0);
27
28      for (;;) {  // Run forever, receiving and echoing datagrams
29        try {
```

```
30          // Receive a byte array with echo datagram packet contents
31          byte[] byteBuffer = client.Receive(ref remoteIPEndPoint);
32          Console.Write("Handling client at " + remoteIPEndPoint + " - ");
33
34          // Send an echo packet back to the client
35          client.Send(byteBuffer, byteBuffer.Length, remoteIPEndPoint);
36          Console.WriteLine("echoed {0} bytes.", byteBuffer.Length);
37        } catch (SocketException se) {
38          Console.WriteLine(se.ErrorCode + ": " + se.Message);
39        }
40      }
41    }
42  }
```

UdpEchoServer.cs

1. **Application setup and parameter parsing:** lines 8–14
   UdpEchoServer takes a single optional parameter, the local port of the echo server socket. The default port used is 7.

2. **Create a UdpClient instance:** lines 16–22
   Unlike our UDP client program, a UDP server must explicitly set its local port to a number known by the client; otherwise, the client will not know the destination port for its echo request datagram. This version of the constructor can throw a SocketException if there is an error when accessing the socket or an ArgumentOutOfRangeException if the port is not within the valid range.

3. **Create an** IPEndPoint **instance:** lines 24–26
   The IPEndPoint class specifies an address and port combination. This IPEndPoint instance will be passed as a reference to the Receive() method, which will populate it with the remote sender's IP address and port information.

4. **Iteratively handle echo request datagrams:** lines 28–40
   The UDP server uses a single UdpClient (and hence a single underlying socket) for all communication, unlike the TCP server which creates a new socket with every successful AcceptTcpClient() or AcceptSocket().

   ▪ **Receive echo request:** line 31
   The Receive() method of UdpClient blocks until a datagram is received from a client (unless a timeout is set). There is no connection, so each datagram may be from a different sender. We receive the incoming packet into a byte array that will also be used to send the echo reply. When the call to Receive() returns, the reference to the IPEndPoint instance is populated with the source's (client's) address and port information.

■ **Send echo reply:** line 35
byteBuffer already contains the echo string and *remoteIPEndPoint* already contains the echo reply destination address and port, so the Send() method of UdpClient can simply transmit the datagram previously received.

UdpClient

Description

Provides User Datagram Protocol (UDP) network services.

Selected Constructors

public UdpClient();

public UdpClient(**int** *port*);

public UdpClient(**IPEndPoint** *localEP*);

public UdpClient(**string** *host name*, **int** *port*);
Creates a new instance of the UdpClient class. The UdpClient constructor has optional arguments for the port, a local interface to bind to (IPEndPoint), or the server to connect to (string host name/IP and integer port). If the destination is not set in the constructor, it must be set either in a Connect() call or in the Send() method. Throws ArgumentNullException, ArgumentException, SocketException.

Selected Methods

public void Close();
Closes the UDP connection. Throws SocketException.

public void Connect(**IPEndPoint** *endPoint*);

public void Connect(**IPAddress** *addr*, **int** *port*);

public void Connect(**string** *host name*, **int** *port*);
Connect() sets the default destination for this UdpClient. This call is optional. Throws ArgumentNullException, ArgumentOutOfRangeException, SocketException, ObjectDisposedException.

public byte[] Receive(**ref IPEndPoint** *remoteEP*);
Returns a UDP datagram sent by a remote host as an byte array and populates the IPEndPoint reference with the endpoint information for the sending remote host. Throws SocketException, ObjectDisposedException.

public int Send(**byte**[] *dgram*, **int** *length*);

public int Send(**byte**[] *dgram*, **int** *length*, **IPEndPoint** *endPoint*);

public int Send(**byte**[] *dgram*, **int** *length*, **string** *host name*, **int** *port*);
Sends a UDP datagram to a remote host. The datagram to send is specified by the byte array argument and the number of bytes to send integer argument. Optional arguments can be included to specify the datagram destination, either using an IPEndPoint instance, or a string host name/IP address and integer port argument. If no default destination has been specified by the UdpClient constructor or Connect() method, the destination is not optional. If a default destination has been set in the constructor or Connect(), you may not use different destination arguments in the Send() call. Returns the number of bytes sent. Throws ArgumentException, InvalidOperationException, SocketException, ObjectDisposedException.

Selected Properties

protected Socket Client {get; set;}
Gets or sets the underlying network socket. Since this is a protected property, it can only be accessed by classes that extend UdpClient. This is useful for accessing socket options that are not directly accessible from the UdpClient API.

2.4.3   Sending and Receiving with UDP Sockets

A subtle but important difference between TCP and UDP is that UDP preserves message boundaries. Each call to UdpClient.Receive() returns data from at most one call to UdpClient.Send(). Moreover, different calls to UdpClient.Receive() will never return data from the same call to UdpClient.Send().

When a call to Write() on a TCP socket's stream returns, all the caller knows is that the data has been copied into a buffer for transmission; the data may or may not have actually been transmitted yet (this is covered in more detail in Chapter 5). UDP, however, does not provide recovery from network errors and, therefore, does not buffer data for possible retransmission. This means that by the time a call to Send() returns, the message has been passed to the underlying channel for transmission and is (or soon will be) on its way out the door.

Between the time a message arrives from the network and the time its data is returned via Read() or Receive(), the data is stored in a *first-in, first-out (FIFO)* queue of received data. With a connected TCP socket, all received-but-not-yet-delivered bytes are treated as one continuous sequence of bytes (see Chapter 5). For a UDP socket, however, the received data may have come from different senders. A UDP socket's received data is kept in a queue of messages, each with associated information identifying its source. A call to Receive() will never return more than one message. The maximum amount of data that can be transmitted by a UdpClient is 65,507 bytes—the largest payload that can be carried in a UDP datagram.

2.5 The .NET Socket Class

The .NET Framework provides a Socket class that is a wrapper around the WinSock implementation. Since TcpClient, TcpListener, and UdpClient all utilize the Socket class for their own implementations, Socket contains all the functionality of those classes, plus much more. The Socket interface is a generic API that actually covers more than just IP, and as such exploring all of the functionality it provides is beyond the scope of this book. In this section we introduce its usage for TCP and UDP and walk through some common cases where you might use it.

2.5.1 TCP Client with Socket

For a TCP client to use the Socket class, it will perform the following steps:

1. **Call the** Socket **constructor:** The constructor specifies the address type, socket type, and protocol type.

2. **Call the** Socket Connect() **method:** Connect() takes an IPEndPoint argument that represents the server to connect to.

3. **Send and receive data:** Using the Socket Send() and Receive() calls.

4. **Close the socket:** Using the Socket Close() method.

Here we present a version of the TcpEchoClient.cs program that uses the Socket class instead of the TcpClient class.

TcpEchoClientSocket.cs

```
0  using System;              // For String, Int32, Console, ArgumentException
1  using System.Text;         // For Encoding
2  using System.IO;           // For IOException
3  using System.Net.Sockets;  // For Socket, SocketException
4  using System.Net;          // For IPAddress, IPEndPoint
5
6  class TcpEchoClientSocket {
7
8    static void Main(string[] args) {
9
10     if ((args.Length < 2) || (args.Length > 3)) { // Test for correct # of args
11       throw new ArgumentException("Parameters: <Server> <Word> [<Port>]");
12     }
13
14     String server = args[0];     // Server name or IP address
15
```

```
16      // Convert input String to bytes
17      byte[] byteBuffer = Encoding.ASCII.GetBytes(args[1]);
18
19      // Use port argument if supplied, otherwise default to 7
20      int servPort = (args.Length == 3) ? Int32.Parse(args[2]) : 7;
21
22      Socket sock = null;
23
24      try {
25        // Create a TCP socket instance
26        sock = new Socket(AddressFamily.InterNetwork, SocketType.Stream,
27                          ProtocolType.Tcp);
28
29        // Creates server IPEndPoint instance. We assume Resolve returns
30        // at least one address
31        IPEndPoint serverEndPoint = new IPEndPoint(Dns.Resolve(server).AddressList[0],
32                                                   servPort);
33        // Connect the socket to server on specified port
34        sock.Connect(serverEndPoint);
35        Console.WriteLine("Connected to server... sending echo string");
36
37        // Send the encoded string to the server
38        sock.Send(byteBuffer, 0, byteBuffer.Length, SocketFlags.None);
39
40        Console.WriteLine("Sent {0} bytes to server...", byteBuffer.Length);
41
42        int totalBytesRcvd = 0;   // Total bytes received so far
43        int bytesRcvd = 0;        // Bytes received in last read
44
45        // Receive the same string back from the server
46        while (totalBytesRcvd < byteBuffer.Length) {
47          if ((bytesRcvd = sock.Receive(byteBuffer, totalBytesRcvd,
48              byteBuffer.Length - totalBytesRcvd, SocketFlags.None)) == 0) {
49            Console.WriteLine("Connection closed prematurely.");
50            break;
51          }
52          totalBytesRcvd += bytesRcvd;
53        }
54
55        Console.WriteLine("Received {0} bytes from server: {1}", totalBytesRcvd,
56                          Encoding.ASCII.GetString(byteBuffer, 0, totalBytesRcvd));
57
58      } catch (Exception e) {
```

```
59          Console.WriteLine(e.Message);
60      } finally {
61          sock.Close();
62      }
63    }
64  }
```

1. **Setup and parameter parsing:** lines 10–22

2. **TCP** Socket **constructor:** lines 25–27
   The Socket constructor takes three arguments:
   - **The address family:** Set to AddressFamily.InterNetwork for IP.
   - **The socket type:** Indicates stream or datagram semantics and is set to Socket-Type.Stream for TCP or SocketType.Dgram for UDP.
   - **The protocol type:** Set to ProtocolType.Tcp or ProtocolType.Udp.

3. **Connect to the server:** lines 29–35
   The Connect() method takes an IPEndPoint instance, which we have constructed from the arguments to the program using IPAddress.Parse(). If the connection fails a SocketException will be thrown.

4. **Send the string to the echo server:** lines 37–38
   The Socket class has several Send() methods that take different combination of parameters, always including a byte array containing the data to be transmitted. Here we use a version that takes (1) the byte buffer containing the data to be sent, (2) the byte offset into the buffer where the data to be sent starts, (3) a total number of bytes to send, and (4) any socket flag settings. Socket flags are beyond the scope of this book, and in this case are set to SocketFlags.None.

5. **Receive the reply from the echo server:** lines 45–53
   Since we know the number of bytes to expect from the echo server, we can repeatedly receive bytes until we have received the same number of bytes that we sent. The Receive() method can be called in several forms; here we use the one that takes four parameters: (1) buffer to receive to, (2) byte offset into the buffer where the first byte received should be placed, (3) the maximum number of bytes to be placed in the buffer, and (4) the socket flags parameter. The loop and data receive logic are identical to those in the earlier TcpClient example.

6. **Print echoed string:** lines 55–56

7. **Error handling and socket close:** lines 58–62

2.5.2   TCP Server with Socket

For a TCP server to use the Socket class, it will perform the following steps:

1. **Call the** Socket **constructor:** The constructor specifies the address type, socket type, and protocol type.

2. **Call the** Socket Bind() **method:** Bind() associates the socket with a local address and port number.

3. **Call the** Socket Listen() **method:** Listen() takes an integer argument representing the number of connections allowed to queue, and starts listening for incoming connections.

4. Repeatedly:

   - **Call the** Socket Accept() **method to accept an incoming connection:** Accept() takes no arguments and returns a Socket instance representing the remote client socket.

   - **Receive and send data:** Using the accepted client Socket instance, use its Receive() and Send() methods to transfer data.

   - **Close the client socket:** Using the Socket Close() method.

5. **Close the server socket:** Using the Socket Close() method.

Here we present a version of the TcpEchoServer.cs program that uses the Socket class instead of the TcpListener and TcpClient classes.

TcpEchoServerSocket.cs

```
0   using System;              // For Console, Int32, ArgumentException, Environment
1   using System.Net;         // For IPAddress
2   using System.Net.Sockets; // For TcpListener, TcpClient
3
4   class TcpEchoServerSocket {
5
6     private const int BUFSIZE = 32; // Size of receive buffer
7     private const int BACKLOG = 5;  // Outstanding connection queue max size
8
9     static void Main(string[] args) {
10
11       if (args.Length > 1) // Test for correct # of args
12         throw new ArgumentException("Parameters: [<Port>]");
13
14       int servPort = (args.Length == 1) ? Int32.Parse(args[0]): 7;
15
```

```
16       Socket server = null;
17
18       try {
19         // Create a socket to accept client connections
20         server = new Socket(AddressFamily.InterNetwork, SocketType.Stream,
21                             ProtocolType.Tcp);
22
23         server.Bind(new IPEndPoint(IPAddress.Any, servPort));
24
25         server.Listen(BACKLOG);
26       } catch (SocketException se) {
27         Console.WriteLine(se.ErrorCode + ": " + se.Message);
28         Environment.Exit(se.ErrorCode);
29       }
30
31       byte[] rcvBuffer = new byte[BUFSIZE]; // Receive buffer
32       int bytesRcvd;                        // Received byte count
33
34       for (;;) { // Run forever, accepting and servicing connections
35
36         Socket client = null;
37
38         try {
39           client = server.Accept(); // Get client connection
40
41           Console.Write("Handling client at " + client.RemoteEndPoint + " - ");
42
43           // Receive until client closes connection, indicated by 0 return value
44           int totalBytesEchoed = 0;
45           while ((bytesRcvd = client.Receive(rcvBuffer, 0, rcvBuffer.Length,
46                                              SocketFlags.None)) > 0) {
47             client.Send(rcvBuffer, 0, bytesRcvd, SocketFlags.None);
48             totalBytesEchoed += bytesRcvd;
49           }
50           Console.WriteLine("echoed {0} bytes.", totalBytesEchoed);
51
52           client.Close();   // Close the socket. We are done with this client!
53
54         } catch (Exception e) {
55           Console.WriteLine(e.Message);
56           client.Close();
57         }
58       }
```

```
59    }
60  }
```

TcpEchoServerSocket.cs

1. **Application setup and parameter parsing:** lines 11–16

2. **Call the** Socket **constructor:** lines 19–21
   The Socket constructor takes three arguments:
   - **The address family:** Set to AddressFamily.InterNetwork for IP.
   - **The socket type:** Indicates stream or datagram semantics and is set to Socket-Type.Stream for TCP or SocketType.Dgram for UDP.
   - **The protocol type:** Set to ProtocolType.Tcp or ProtocolType.Udp.

3. **Bind the socket:** line 23
   The Bind() method is called with a IPEndPoint instance containing IPAddress.Any (0.0.0.0) and the specified server port number. The bind assigns the socket a local address and port and throws a SocketException if it fails to do so (e.g., if the local endpoint is already in use).

4. **Listen for incoming connections:** line 25
   The Listen() method causes the socket to begin handling incoming TCP connection requests and queuing them for acceptance by our program. It takes an integer argument that specifies the *backlog*, which is the maximum number of outstanding connections allowed in the queue. The valid values for the backlog are typically 1–5, but may vary by system; check your documentation.

5. **Loop forever, iteratively handling incoming connections:** lines 34–58
   - **Accept an incoming connection:** line 39
     The server Socket instance supplies new, connected client Socket instances for each new TCP connection. When the server is ready to handle a client, it calls Accept(), which blocks until an incoming connection is made to the server Socket's port. Accept() then returns an instance of Socket that is already *connected* to the remote socket and ready for reading and writing.
   - **Output the remote end point being serviced:** line 41
     One feature of Socket that is not available with TcpClient is the ability to access the RemoteEndPoint property and determine the IP address and port of the client connection.
   - **Receive and repeat data until the client closes:** lines 43–50
     The while loop repeatedly reads bytes (when available) from the Socket and immediately writes the same bytes back to the stream until the client closes the connection. The loop and data transfer logic are identical to the TcpClient version.

- **Close the client socket:** line 52
- **Exception handling:** lines 54–57

Socket

Description

The Socket class is a wrapper around the WinSock sockets API. Using a Socket involves the following steps:

1. Create a Socket instance with the socket constructor.
2. If the Socket is a server, call Bind() to assign a local endpoint.
3. If the Socket is a client, call Connect() to connect to a remote endpoint.
4. If the Socket is a server, call Listen() to begin listening for connections, and call Accept() to retrieve an incoming connection.
5. Use the Send() and Receive() methods to transfer data over TCP, or SendTo() and ReceiveFrom() for UDP.
6. Call Shutdown() to disable the socket.
7. Call Close() to close the socket.

Constructor

public Socket(**AddressFamily**, **SocketType**, **ProtocolType**);
Creates a new instance of the Socket class. Each argument is specified by its own enumeration class, AddressFamily, SocketType, and ProtocolType. For the purposes of this book, the AddressFamily is set to InterNetwork, the SocketType is set to Stream for TCP semantics or Dgram for UDP semantics, and the ProtocolType is set to Tcp for TCP and Udp for UDP.

Selected Methods

public void Bind(**EndPoint** *localEP*);
Associates a Socket with a local endpoint. Throws ArgumentNullException, Socket-Exception, ObjectDisposedException.

public void Close();
Closes a Socket connection.

public void Connect(**EndPoint** *remoteEP*);
Establishes a connection to a remote server. Throws ArgumentNullException, Socket-Exception, ObjectDisposedException.

public object GetSocketOption(**SocketOptionLevel, SocketOptionName**);

public void GetSocketOption(**SocketOptionLevel, SocketOptionName, byte**[]);

public byte[] GetSocketOption(**SocketOptionLevel, SocketOptionName, int**);
Returns the value of the specified Socket option in an object or in an array of bytes. The complete list of properties available for SocketOptionLevel and SocketOptionName are detailed in their respective class descriptions following this class. Throws SocketException, ObjectDisposedException.

public void Listen(**int** *backlog*);
Changes the Socket state to handle incoming TCP connections and queue them to be accepted by the program. The *backlog* specifies the maximum number of incoming connections that can be queued at any time. The normal *backlog* values are 1–5 but vary by system; check your documentation. Throws SocketException, ObjectDisposedException.

public bool Poll(**int** *microseconds*, **SelectMode** *mode*);
Checks the status of a Socket. The first argument specifies the number of microseconds to wait for a response. A negative value indicates blocking indefinitely. The status checked depends on the SelectMode enumeration argument. SelectMode.SelectRead checks for readability. SelectMode.SelectWrite checks for writeability. SelectMode.SelectError checks for the existence of an error.

public int Receive(**byte**[] *buffer*);

public int Receive(**byte**[] *buffer*, **SocketFlags** *flags*);

public int Receive(**byte**[] *buffer*, **int** *length*, **SocketFlags** *flags*);

public int Receive(**byte**[] *buffer*, **int** *offset*, **int** *length*, **SocketFlags** *flags*);
Receives data from the Socket into the byte buffer argument. Optional arguments include SocketFlags, an integer number of bytes to receive, and an integer offset in the buffer. Returns the number of bytes received. Throws ArgumentNullException, ArgumentOutOfRangeException, SocketException, ObjectDisposedException.

public int ReceiveFrom(**byte**[] *buffer*, **ref EndPoint** *remoteEP*);

public int ReceiveFrom(**byte**[] *buffer*, **SocketFlags** *flags*, **ref EndPoint** *remoteEP*);

public int ReceiveFrom(**byte**[] *buffer*, **int** *length*, **SocketFlags** *flags*, **ref EndPoint** *remoteEP*);

public int ReceiveFrom(**byte**[] *buffer*, **int** *offset*, **int** *length*, **SocketFlags** *flags*, **ref EndPoint** *localEP*);
Receives a UDP datagram into the byte buffer argument and populates the EndPoint reference with the sender's endpoint information. Optional arguments include SocketFlags, an integer number of bytes to receive, and an integer offset in the buffer. Returns the number of bytes received. Note that there is an important difference between the byte buffer used to receive datagrams with a Socket and a UdpClient. While the UdpClient returns a reference to preallocated buffer, the

Socket class requires the buffer argument to be preallocated to the appropriate size. If an attempt is made to receive more bytes into the buffer argument than has been allocated, a SocketException will be thrown with the ErrorCode set to 10040 (WinSock constant WSAEMSGSIZE), and the Message set to "Message too long." Throws ArgumentNullException, ArgumentOutOfRangeException, SocketException, ObjectDisposedException.

public static void Select(**IList** *readableList*, **IList** *writeableList*, **IList** *errorList*, **int** *microseconds*);
Used to determine the status of one or more Socket instances. This method takes between one and three IList container types holding Socket instances (lists not passed should be set to null). What is checked for depends on the IList's position in the argument list. The Sockets in the first IList are checked for readability. The Sockets in the second IList are checked for writeability. The Sockets in the third IList are checked for errors. After completing, only the Socket instances that meet the criteria will still be in the IList. The final argument is the time in microseconds to wait for a response. Throws ArgumentNullException, SocketException.

public int Send(**byte**[] *buffer*);

public int Send(**byte**[] *buffer*, **SocketFlags** *flags*);

public int Send(**byte**[] *buffer*, **int** *length*, **SocketFlags** *flags*);

public int Send(**byte**[] *buffer*, **int** *offset*, **int** *length*, **SocketFlags** *flags*);
Sends data to the Socket from the byte buffer argument. Optional arguments include SocketFlags, an integer number of bytes to send, and an integer offset in the buffer. Returns the number of bytes sent. Throws ArgumentNullException, ArgumentOutOfRangeException, SocketException, ObjectDisposedException.

public int SendTo(**byte**[] *buffer*, **EndPoint** *remoteEP*);

public int SendTo(**byte**[] *buffer*, **SocketFlags** *flags*, **EndPoint** *remoteEP*);

public int SendTo(**byte**[] *buffer*, **int** *length*, **SocketFlags** *flags*, **EndPoint** *remoteEP*);

public int SendTo(**byte**[] *buffer*, **int** *offset*, **int** *length*, **SocketFlags** *flags*, **EndPoint** *remoteEP*);
Sends a UDP datagram packet specified in the byte buffer argument to a specific endpoint. Optional arguments include SocketFlags, an integer number of bytes to send, and an integer offset in the buffer. Returns the number of bytes sent. Throws ArgumentNullException, ArgumentOutOfRangeException, SocketException, ObjectDisposedException.

public void SetSocketOption(**SocketOptionLevel** *optionLevel*, **SocketOptionName** *optionName*, **byte**[] *optionValue*);

public void SetSocketOption(**SocketOptionLevel** *optionLevel*, **SocketOptionName** *optionName*, **int** *optionValue*);

public void SetSocketOption(**SocketOptionLevel** *optionLevel*, **SocketOptionName** *optionName*, **object** *optionValue*);
Sets the specified socket option to the specified value. The complete list of properties available for SocketOptionLevel and SocketOptionName are detailed in their respective class descriptions following this class. Throws ArgumentNullException, SocketException, ObjectDisposedException.

public void Shutdown(**SocketShutdown** *how*);
Disables sends and/or receives on a Socket. The argument is a SocketShutdown enumeration indicating what should be shutdown (**Send**, **Receive**, or **Both**). Throws SocketException, ObjectDisposedException.

Selected Properties

public bool Connected {get;}
Gets a value indicating whether a Socket is connected to a remote resource *as of the most recent I/O operation.*

public EndPoint LocalEndPoint {get;}
Gets the local endpoint that the Socket is bound to for communications.

public EndPoint RemoteEndPoint {get;}
Gets the remote endpoint that the Socket is using for communication.

SocketOptionLevel

Description

The SocketOptionLevel enumeration defines the level that a socket option should be applied to. A SocketOptionLevel is input to the Socket.SetSocketOption() and Socket.GetSocketOption() methods.

Members

IP	Socket options apply to IP sockets.
Socket	Socket options apply to the socket itself.
Tcp	Socket options apply to TCP sockets.
Udp	Socket options apply to UDP sockets.

SocketOptionName

Description

The SocketOptionName enumeration defines socket option names for the Socket class and is passed as input to the Socket.SetSocketOption() and Socket.GetSocket-Option() methods. Socket options are described in more detail in Section 2.5.4, but coverage of all of the socket options is beyond the scope of this book. Check *www.msdn.microsoft.com* for more details on these options.

Members

See Table 2.1 for a list of available .NET socket options. Note that at the time this book went to press there was not sufficient documentation to determine if all of these socket options were fully supported and/or implemented. Check the MSDN library at *www.msdn.microsoft.com/library* for the latest information.

SocketFlags

Description

The SocketFlags enumeration provides the valid values for advanced socket flags and is an optional input to the Socket data transfer methods. If you need to use a Socket method that requires a socket flag argument but don't need any flags set, use SocketFlags.None. See Section 2.5.5 for more on socket flags.

Members

DontRoute	Send without using routing tables.
MaxIOVectorLength	Provides a standard value for the number of WSABUF structures used to send and receive data.
None	Use no flags for this call.
OutOfBand	Process out-of-band data.
Partial	Partial send or receive for message.
Peek	Peek at incoming message.

SocketOptionName	Type	Values	Description
SocketOptionLevel.Socket			
AcceptConnection	Boolean	0, 1	Socket has called Listen(). Get only.
Broadcast	Boolean	0, 1	Broadcast messages allowed.
Debug	Boolean	0, 1	Record debugging information (if available).
DontLinger	Boolean	0, 1	Close socket without waiting for confirmation.
DontRoute	Boolean	0, 1	For multihomed hosts, send using the specified outgoing interface instead of routing.
Error	Int32	WinSock error code	Get and clear the socket error code (see Appendix). Get only.
ExclusiveAddressUse	Boolean	0, 1	Enables a socket to be bound for exclusive access.
KeepAlive	Boolean	0, 1	Keep-alive messages enabled (if implemented by the protocol).
Linger	LingerOption	0, 1; seconds	Time to delay Close() return waiting for confirmation.
MaxConnections	Int32	max size	Maximum queue length that can be specified by Socket.Listen(). Get only.
OutOfBandInline	Boolean	0, 1	Receives out-of-band data in the normal data stream.
ReceiveBuffer	Int32	bytes	Bytes in the socket receive buffer.
ReceiveLowWater	Int32	bytes	Minimum number of bytes that will cause Receive() to return.
ReceiveTimeout	Int32	milliseconds	Receive timeout.
ReuseAddress	Boolean	0, 1	Binding allowed (under certain conditions) to an address or port already in use.
SendBuffer	Int32	bytes	Bytes in the socket send buffer.
SendLowWater	Int32	bytes	Minimum bytes to send.
SendTimeout	Int32	milliseconds	Send timeout.
Type	Int32	SocketType	Get socket type. Get only.
SocketOptionLevel.Tcp			
BsdUrgent	Boolean	0, 1	Urgent data as defined in RFC-1122.
Expedited	Boolean	0, 1	Expedited data as defined in RFC-1122.
NoDelay	Boolean	0, 1	Disallow delay for data merging (Nagle's algorithm).

SocketOptionLevel.Udp

ChecksumCoverage	Boolean	0, 1	Get/set UDP checksum coverage.
NoChecksum	Boolean	0, 1	UDP datagrams sent with checksum set to zero.

SocketOptionLevel.IP

AddMembership	MulticastOption	group address, interface	Add a multicast group membership. Set only.
AddSourceMembership	IPAddress	group address	Join a multicast source group. Set only.
BlockSource	Boolean	0, 1	Block data from a multicast source. Set only.
DontFragment	Boolean	0, 1	Do not fragment IP datagrams.
DropMembership	MulticastOption	group address, interface	Drop a multicast group membership. Set only.
DropSourceMembership	IPAddress	group address	Drop a multicast source group. Set only.
HeaderIncluded	Boolean	0, 1	Application is providing the IP header for outgoing datagrams.
IPOptions	Byte[]	IP options	Specifies IP options to be inserted into outgoing datagrams.
IpTimeToLive	Int32	0–255	Set the IP header time-to-live field.
MulticastInterface	Byte[]	interface	Set the interface for outgoing multicast packets.
MulticastLoopback	Boolean	0, 1	IP multicast loopback.
MulticastTimeToLive	Int32	0–255	IP multicast time to live.
PacketInformation	Byte[]	packet info	Return information about received packets. Get only.
TypeOfService	Int32	SocketType	Change the IP header type of service field.
UnblockSource	Boolean	0, 1	Unblock a previously blocked multicast source.
UseLoopback	Boolean	0, 1	Bypass hardware when possible.

Table 2.1: Socket Options

SocketException

Description

SocketException is a subclass of Exception that is thrown when a socket error occurs.

Selected Properties

public override int ErrorCode {get;}
The ErrorCode property contains the error number of the error that has occurred. This is extremely useful since a SocketException can be thrown for many different reasons, and you often need to distinguish which situation has occurred in order to handle it properly. The error number corresponds to the underlying WinSock 2 (Windows implementation of sockets) error codes. See Appendix for more details.

public virtual string Message {get;}
Contains the human-readable text description of the error that has occurred.

2.5.3 TcpListener AcceptSocket()

Notice that in TcpEchoServer.cs we don't report the IP address of the client connection. If you look through the API for TcpClient, you'll notice that there is no way to directly access this information. It certainly would be nice to have the server report the IP addresses/ports of its clients. In TcpEchoServerSocket.cs you can see that the Socket class gives you access to this information in the RemoteEndPoint property.

The TcpListener class provides an alternative accept call to give you access to this client information. The AcceptSocket() method of TcpListener works identically to the AcceptTcpClient() method except that it returns a client Socket instance instead of a client TcpClient instance. Once we obtain the client Socket instance, the remote connection's IP address and port are available via the RemoteEndPoint property. The client Socket is then used just as we have seen in our Socket examples. It does not use a stream class but uses the Socket Send() and Receive() methods to transfer byte arrays. The code in the for loop of TcpEchoServer.cs can be rewritten to use Socket as follows:

```
for (;;) { // Run forever, accepting and servicing connections

    Socket sock = null;

    try {
      // Get client connection as a Socket
      sock = listener.AcceptSocket();
```

```
// Socket property RemoteEndPoint contains the client's address
// and port:
Console.Write("Handling client at " + sock.RemoteEndPoint + " - ");

// Receive until client closes connection, indicated by 0 return value
// Use the Socket methods Receive() and Send()
int totalBytesEchoed = 0;
while ((bytesRcvd = sock.Receive(rcvBuffer, 0, rcvBuffer.Length,
        SocketFlags.None)) > 0) {
  sock.Send(rcvBuffer, 0, bytesRcvd, SocketFlags.None);
  totalBytesEchoed += bytesRcvd;
}
Console.WriteLine("echoed {0} bytes.", totalBytesRcvd);

sock.Close(); // Close the socket, we are done with this client!
} catch (Exception e) {
Console.WriteLine(e.Message);
sock.Close();
}
}
```

This code turns out to be very similar to our TcpClient version. The primary differences are:

- TcpListener's AcceptSocket() method is called instead of AcceptTcpClient().

- The RemoteEndPoint property of the client Socket returns an instance of an EndPoint containing the address of the client. Used in a Write() call, this is converted into a string representation of the IP address and port.

- No NetworkStream is used; the Socket's Send() and Receive() methods are called instead.

- We call Close() on the client Socket instead of the NetworkStream and TcpClient.

2.5.4 Socket Options

The TCP/IP protocol developers spent a good deal of time thinking about the default behaviors that would satisfy most applications. (If you doubt this, read RFCs 1122 [27] and 1123 [28], which describe in excruciating detail the recommended behaviors—based on years of experience—for implementations of the TCP/IP protocols.) For most applications, the designers did a good job; however, it is seldom the case that "one size fits all" really fits all. For just such situations, sockets allows many of its default behaviors to be changed, and these behaviors are called *socket options*. In .NET the level of access to socket options is determined by the class you are using. With instances of TcpListener and UdpClient, you are stuck with the default behaviors. The TcpClient class has a subset of socket options accessible as public properties, listed in Table 2.2.

TcpClient **Property**	**Description**
LingerState	Gets or sets information about the sockets linger time.
NoDelay	Gets or sets a value that disables a delay when send or receive buffers are not full.
ReceiveBufferSize	Gets or sets the size of the receive buffer.
ReceiveTimeout	Gets or sets the amount of time a TcpClient will wait to receive data once a read operation is initiated.
SendBufferSize	Gets or sets the size of the send buffer.
SendTimeout	Gets or sets the amount of time a TcpClient will wait for a send operation to complete successfully.

Table 2.2: Socket Options Available via the Public Properties of the TcpClient Class

For access to all of the available socket options you need to use the Socket class. The Socket class methods GetSocketOption() and SetSocketOption() provide the get and set capabilities for the option. These methods are overloaded to accommodate the data types of the different options, but in all cases they take a socket option name and a socket option level. The socket option name is the name of the option to get/set, and its valid values are provided in the enumeration class SocketOptionName. The full list of all SocketOptionName values is displayed in the SocketOptionName class summary on Table 2.1. Discussing all of these options is beyond the scope of this book. Check Microsoft's documentation at *www.msdn.microsoft.com* for more details. The socket option level is the scope of the option to get/set, such as socket-level, TCP-level, or IP-level. The valid socket option level values are provided in the enumeration class SocketOptionLevel.

The only mechanism to get or set socket options for higher level classes (beyond those exposed in the TcpClient properties) is to access the underlying Socket using a protected property. Since the property is protected, it is only accessible by extending the class. In the future we expect that the more common socket options will be added using public properties and accessor methods to the higher level socket classes.

In UdpEchoClient.cs in Section 2.4.1 we discussed the need to provide a timeout on the Receive() call to prevent hanging indefinitely when a UDP server did not respond or packets were lost. The SocketOptionName.ReceiveTimeout option provides just this functionality. Here we present a modified version of the UDP echo client that illustrates setting a socket option. The modified UDP client uses the ReceiveTimeout socket option to specify a maximum amount of time to block on Receive(), after which it tries again by resending the echo request datagram. Our new echo client performs the following steps:

1. Send the echo string to the server.

2. Block on Receive() for up to three seconds, starting over (up to five times) if the reply is not received before the timeout.

3. Terminate the client.

Since the timeout limit is only available with the Socket class we have two options: code the entire client using the Socket class, or use UdpClient and retrieve the underlying Socket instance when we need to set the timeout. Since the UdpClient.Client property that allows you to access the underlying Socket instance is a protected property, it is not directly accessible unless you created a derived class of UdpClient. For the purposes of illustrating the use of the Socket class for UDP, we have chosen the former approach here.

UdpEchoClientTimeoutSocket.cs

```
0   using System;              // For String, Int32, Boolean, Console
1   using System.Text;         // For Encoding
2   using System.Net;          // For EndPoint, IPEndPoint
3   using System.Net.Sockets;  // For Socket, SocketOptionName, SocketOptionLevel
4
5   class UdpEchoClientTimeout {
6
7     private const int TIMEOUT = 3000; // Resend timeout (milliseconds)
8     private const int MAXTRIES = 5;   // Maximum retransmissions
9
10    static void Main(string[] args) {
11
12      if ((args.Length < 2) || (args.Length > 3)) { // Test for correct # of args
13        throw new ArgumentException("Parameters: <Server> <Word> [<Port>]");
14      }
15
16      String server = args[0];     // Server name or IP address
17
18      // Use port argument if supplied, otherwise default to 7
19      int servPort = (args.Length == 3) ? Int32.Parse(args[2]) : 7;
20
21      // Create socket that is connected to server on specified port
22      Socket sock = new Socket(AddressFamily.InterNetwork,
23                               SocketType.Dgram, ProtocolType.Udp);
24
25      // Set the receive timeout for this socket
26      sock.SetSocketOption(SocketOptionLevel.Socket,
27                           SocketOptionName.ReceiveTimeout, TIMEOUT);
28
29      IPEndPoint remoteIPEndPoint = new
30                      IPEndPoint(Dns.Resolve(server).AddressList[0], servPort);
31      EndPoint remoteEndPoint = (EndPoint)remoteIPEndPoint;
```

```
32
33     // Convert input String to a packet of bytes
34     byte[] sendPacket = Encoding.ASCII.GetBytes(args[1]);
35     byte[] rcvPacket = new byte[sendPacket.Length];
36
37     int tries = 0;   // Packets may be lost, so we have to keep trying
38     Boolean receivedResponse = false;
39
40     do {
41       sock.SendTo(sendPacket, remoteEndPoint);   // Send the echo string
42
43       Console.WriteLine("Sent {0} bytes to the server...", sendPacket.Length);
44
45       try {
46         // Attempt echo reply receive
47         sock.ReceiveFrom(rcvPacket, ref remoteEndPoint);
48         receivedResponse = true;
49       } catch (SocketException se) {
50         tries++;
51         if (se.ErrorCode == 10060) // WSAETIMEDOUT: Connection timed out
52           Console.WriteLine("Timed out, {0} more tries...", (MAXTRIES - tries));
53         else // We encountered an error other than a timeout, output error message
54           Console.WriteLine(se.ErrorCode + ": " + se.Message);
55       }
56     } while ((!receivedResponse) && (tries < MAXTRIES));
57
58     if (receivedResponse)
59       Console.WriteLine("Received {0} bytes from {1}: {2}",
60                         rcvPacket.Length, remoteEndPoint,
61                         Encoding.ASCII.GetString(rcvPacket, 0, rcvPacket.Length));
62     else
63       Console.WriteLine("No response -- giving up.");
64
65     sock.Close();
66   }
67 }
```

UdpEchoClientTimeoutSocket.cs

1. **Application setup and parameter parsing:** lines 12–19

2. **UDP socket creation:** lines 21–23
   The Socket constructor takes three arguments:
   - **The address family:** Set to AddressFamily.InterNetwork for IP.
   - **The socket type:** Indicates stream or datagram semantics and is set to Socket-Type.Dgram for UDP.
   - **The protocol type:** Set to ProtocolType.Udp.

3. **Set the socket timeout:** lines 25–27
   The timeout for a datagram socket controls the maximum amount of time (in milliseconds) that a call to Receive() will block. The socket option level is Socket-OptionLevel.Socket. The SetSocketOption() method with the argument Socket-OptionName.ReceiveTimeout is used to set the receiving timeout. The third argument is the timeout duration, which we set to three seconds (3000 milliseconds). Note that timeouts are not precise: the call may block for more than the specified time (but not less).

4. **Create the destination address structure:** lines 29–31
   The destination argument data structure is an instance of the class EndPoint. In this case, we create an instance of the subclass IPEndPoint, which contains methods that will resolve our IP addresses for us, and then cast it to the EndPoint class. In order to resolve any host name that was input, we first call Dns.Resolve(). We then use the first IPAddress instance returned by that call as the input to the IPEndPoint constructor, along with the port number from the command line.

5. **Create datagram to send:** lines 33–34
   Convert the argument to a byte array.

6. **Create datagram to receive:** line 35
   To create a datagram for receiving, we only need to specify a byte array to hold the datagram data. In this case we know the exact size of the packet that we are expecting, which is the same size as the packet we sent.

7. **Send the datagram:** lines 37–56
   The Socket class uses UDP specific methods for sending and receiving called SendTo() and ReceiveFrom(). Since datagrams may be lost, we must be prepared to retransmit the datagram. We loop sending and attempting a receive of the echo reply up to five times.
   - **Send the datagram:** line 41
     The Socket class uses the SendTo() method for transmitting the datagram to the address and port specified in the specified EndPoint.
   - **Handle datagram reception:** lines 45–56
     ReceiveFrom() blocks until it either receives a datagram or the timer expires. Timer expiration is indicated by a SocketException with the ErrorCode property set to 10060 with a Message of "connection timed out" (see the Appendix for more

on ErrorCode). If the timer expires, we increment the send attempt count (*tries*) and start over. After the maximum number of tries, the while loop exits without receiving the datagram. If Receive() succeeds, we set the loop flag *receivedResponse* to **true**, causing the loop to exit.

8. **Print reception results:** lines 58–63

   If we received a datagram, *receivedResponse* is **true**, and we can print the datagram data.

9. **Close the socket:** line 65

2.5.5   Socket Flags

The SocketFlags enumeration provides some additional ways to alter the default behavior of individual Send()/SendTo() and Receive()/ReceiveFrom() calls. To use socket flags the appropriate flag enumeration is simply passed as an argument to the send or receive method. Although it is beyond the scope of this book to describe all the socket flags available (see page 47 for a list), we present a simple code example here for SocketFlags.Peek.

Peek allows you to view the contents of the next Receive()/ ReceiveFrom() without actually dequeuing the results from the network-system buffer. What this means is that you can create a copy of the contents of the next read, but the subsequent read will return the same bytes again.[3] In theory this can be used to check the contents of the next read and have the application make a decision on what to do based on that advance knowledge. In practice, this is extremely inefficient (and, indeed, not always reliable [22]), and it is almost always better to read the contents first and decide what to do with them afterwards. However, we have included a code snippet here to illustrate the use of SocketFlags:

```
Socket s = new Socket(AddressFamily.InterNetwork, SocketType.Stream,
                      ProtocolType.Tcp);

// Bind and/or Connect, create buffer
:

// Peek at the data without dequeuing it from the network buffer
int len = s.Receive(buf, 0, buf.Length, SocketFlags.Peek);

// This Receive will return (at least) the same data as the prior
// Receive, but this time it will be dequeued from the network buffer
len = s.Receive(buf, 0, buf.Length, SocketFlags.None);
```

---

[3] In fact, if more bytes have been received over the network since the peek, the subsequent read might return more data than the peek. The point is that unlike a nonpeek read, the bytes returned were not removed from the buffer and are still available to be read again.

See TcpEchoPeekClient.cs on the book's website (www.mtp.com/practical/ csharpsockets) for an implementation of the echo client that peeks at the echo reply prior to dequeuing it.

2.6 Exercises

1. For TcpEchoServer.cs, we explicitly specify the port to the socket in the constructor. We said that a socket must have a port for communication, yet we do not specify a port in TcpEchoClient.cs. How is the echo client's socket assigned a port?

2. When you make a phone call, it is usually the callee that answers with "Hello." What changes to our client and server example would be needed to implement this?

3. What happens if a TCP server never calls an accept method (Accept(), Accept-Socket(), or AcceptTcpClient())? What happens if a TCP client sends data on a socket that has not yet been accepted at the server?

4. Servers are supposed to run for a long time without stopping—therefore, they must be designed to provide good service no matter what their clients do. Examine the server in the examples (TcpEchoServer.cs and UdpEchoServer.cs) and list anything you can think of that a client might do to cause it to give poor service to other clients. Suggest improvements to fix the problems that you find.

5. Modify TcpEchoServer.cs to read and write only a single byte at a time, sleeping one second between each byte. Verify that TcpEchoClient.cs requires multiples reads to successfully receive the entire echo string, even though it sent the echo string with one Write().

6. Modify TcpEchoServer.cs to read and write a single byte and then close the socket. What happens when the TcpEchoClient sends a multibyte string to this server? What is happening?

7. Modify UdpEchoServer.cs so that it only echoes every other datagram it receives. Verify that UdpEchoClientTimeoutSocket.cs retransmits datagrams until it either receives a reply or exceeds the number of retries.

8. Verify experimentally the size of the largest message you can send and receive using UDP.

9. While UdpEchoServer.cs explicitly specifies its local port in the constructor, we do not specify the local port in UdpEchoClientTimeoutSocket.cs. How is the UDP echo client's socket given a port number? (Hint: The answer is different than the answer for TCP.)

Sending and Receiving Messages

When writing programs to communicate via sockets, you will generally be implementing an *application protocol* of some sort. Typically you use sockets because your program needs to provide information to, or use information provided by, another program. There is no magic: Sender and receiver must agree on how this information will be encoded, who sends what information when, and how the communication will be terminated. In our echo example, the application protocol is trivial: neither the client's nor the server's behavior is affected by the *contents* of the bytes they exchange. Because most applications require that the behaviors of client and server depend upon the *information* they exchange, application protocols are usually more complicated.

The TCP/IP protocols transport bytes of user data without examining or modifying them. This allows applications great flexibility in how they encode their information for transmission. For various reasons, most application protocols are defined in terms of discrete *messages* made up of sequences of *fields*. Each field contains a specific piece of information encoded as a sequence of bits. The application protocol specifies exactly how these sequences of bits are to be formatted by the sender and interpreted, or *parsed*, by the receiver so that the latter can extract the meaning of each field. About the only constraint imposed by TCP/IP is that information must be sent and received in chunks whose length in bits is a multiple of eight. From now on, then, we consider messages to be sequences of *bytes*. Given this, it may be helpful to think of a transmitted message as a sequence of numbers, each between 0 and 255 inclusive (that being the range of binary values that can be encoded in 8 bits—1 byte).

As a concrete example for this chapter, let's consider the problem of transferring price quote information between vendors and buyers. A simple quote for some quantity of a particular item might include the following information:

Item number: A large integer identifying the item

Item description: A text string describing the item

Unit price: The cost per item in cents

Quantity: The number of units offered at that price

Discounted?: Whether the price includes a discount

In stock?: Whether the item is in stock

We collect this information in a class ItemQuote.cs. For convenience in viewing the information in our program examples, we include a ToString() method. Throughout this chapter, the variable *item* refers to an instance of ItemQuote.

ItemQuote.cs

```
0  using System;  // For String and Boolean
1
2  public class ItemQuote {
3
4    public long itemNumber;         // Item identification number
5    public String itemDescription;  // String description of item
6    public int quantity;            // Number of items in quote (always >= 1)
7    public int unitPrice;           // Price (in cents) per item
8    public Boolean discounted;      // Price reflect a discount?
9    public Boolean inStock;         // Item(s) ready to ship?
10
11   public ItemQuote() {}
12
13   public ItemQuote(long itemNumber, String itemDescription,
14           int quantity, int unitPrice, Boolean discounted, Boolean inStock) {
15     this.itemNumber      = itemNumber;
16     this.itemDescription = itemDescription;
17     this.quantity        = quantity;
18     this.unitPrice       = unitPrice;
19     this.discounted      = discounted;
20     this.inStock         = inStock;
21   }
22
23   public override String ToString() {
24     String EOLN = "\n";
25     String value = "Item# = " + itemNumber + EOLN +
26                    "Description = " + itemDescription + EOLN +
```

```
27                    "Quantity = " + quantity + EOLN +
28                    "Price (each) = " + unitPrice + EOLN +
29                    "Total Price = " + (quantity * unitPrice);
30
31     if (discounted)
32       value += " (discounted)";
33     if (inStock)
34       value += EOLN + "In Stock" + EOLN;
35     else
36       value += EOLN + "Out of Stock" + EOLN;
37
38     return value;
39   }
40 }
```

ItemQuote.cs

3.1 Encoding Information

What if a client program needs to obtain quote information from a vendor program? The two programs must agree on how the information contained in the ItemQuote will be represented as a sequence of bytes "on the wire"—sent over a TCP connection or carried in a UDP datagram. (Note that everything in this chapter also applies if the "wire" is a file that is written by one program and read by another.) In our example, the information to be represented consists of integers, Booleans, and a character string.

Transmitting information via the network in the .NET framework requires that it be written to a NetworkStream (of a TcpClient or TcpListener) or written in a byte array to a Socket or UdpClient. What this means is that the only data types to which these operations can be applied are **byte**s and arrays of **byte**s. As a strongly typed language, C# requires that other types—String, **int**, and so on—be explicitly converted to these transmittable types. Fortunately, the language has a number of built-in facilities that make such conversions more convenient. Before dealing with the specifics of our example, however, we focus on some basic concepts of representing information as sequences of bytes for transmission.

3.1.1 Text

Old-fashioned text—strings of printable (displayable) characters—is perhaps the most common form of information representation. When the information to be transmitted is natural language, text is the most natural representation. Text is convenient for other forms of information because humans can easily deal with it when printed or displayed; numbers, for example, can be represented as strings of decimal digits.

To send text, the string of characters is translated into a sequence of **byte**s according to a *character set*. The canonical example of a character encoding system is the venerable *American Standard Code for Information Interchange* (ASCII), which defines a one-to-one mapping between a set of the most commonly used printable characters in English and binary values. For example, in ASCII the digit 0 is represented by the byte value 48, 1 by 49, and so on up to 9, which is represented by the byte value 57. ASCII is adequate for applications that only need to exchange English text. As the economy becomes increasingly globalized, however, applications need to deal with other languages, including many that use characters for which ASCII has no encoding, and even some (e.g., Chinese) that use more than 256 characters and thus require more than 1 byte per character to encode. Encodings for the world's languages are defined by companies and by standards bodies. *Unicode* is the most widely recognized such character encoding; it is standardized by the International Organization for Standardization (ISO).

Fortunately, the .NET framework provides good support for internationalization. .NET provides classes that can be used to encode text into ASCII, Unicode, or several variants of Unicode (UTF-7 and UTF-8). Standard Unicode defines a 16-bit (2-byte) code for each character and thus supports a much larger set of characters than ASCII. In fact, the Unicode standard currently defines codes for over 49,000 characters and covers "the principal written languages and symbol systems of the world" [23]. .NET supports a number of additional encodings as well, and provides a clean separation between its internal representation and the encoding used when characters are input or output. The default encoding for C# may vary depending on regional operating system settings but is usually UTF-8, which supports the entire Unicode character set. (UTF-8, also known as USC Transformation Format 8-bit form, encodes characters in 8 bits when possible to save space, utilizing 16 bits only when necessary.) The default encoding is referenced via System.Text.Encoding.Default.

The System.Text encoding classes provide several mechanisms for converting between different character sets. The ASCIIEncoding, UnicodeEncoding, UTF7Encoding, and UTF8-Encoding classes all provide GetBytes() and GetString() methods to convert from String to byte array or vice versa in the specified encoding. The Encoding class also contains static versions of some character set classes (ASCII and Unicode) that contain the same methods. The GetBytes() method returns the sequence of bytes that represent the given string in encoding of the class used. Similarly, the GetString() method of encoding classes takes a byte array and returns a String instance containing the sequence of characters represented by the byte sequence according to the invoked encoding class.

Suppose the value of *item.itemNumber* is 123456. Using ASCII, that part of the string representation of *item* produced by ToString() would be encoded as

105	116	101	109	35	61	49	50	51	52	53	54
'i'	't'	'e'	'm'	'#'	'='	'1'	'2'	'3'	'4'	'5'	'6'

Using the "ISO8859_1" encoding would produce the same sequence of byte values, because the *International Standard 8859-1* encoding (which is also known as *ISO Latin 1*) is an extension of ASCII: It maps the characters of the ASCII set to the same values as ASCII. However, if we used the North American version of IBM's *Extended Binary Coded Decimal Interchange Code* (EBCDIC), the result would be rather different:

137	163	133	148	123	126	241	242	243	244	245	246
'i'	't'	'e'	'm'	'#'	'='	'1'	'2'	'3'	'4'	'5'	'6'

If we used Unicode, the result would use 2 bytes per character, with 1 byte containing zero and the other byte containing the same value as with ASCII. Obviously, the primary requirement in dealing with character encodings is that the sender and receiver must agree on the code to be used.

3.1.2 Binary Numbers

Transmitting large numbers as text strings is not very efficient. Each character in the digit string has one of only 10 values, which can be represented using, on average, less than 4 bits per digit. Yet the standard character codes invariably use at least 8 bits per character. Moreover, it is inconvenient to perform arithmetic computation and comparisons with numbers encoded as strings. For example, a receiving program computing the total cost of a quote (quantity times unit price) will generally need to convert both amounts to the local computer's native (binary) integer representation before the computation can be performed. For a more compact and computation-friendly encoding, we can transmit the values of the integers in our data as binary values. To send binary integers as byte sequences, the sender and receiver need to agree on several things:

- *Integer size:* How many bits are used to represent the integer? The sizes of C#'s integer types are fixed by the language definition—**short**s are 2 bytes, **int**s are 4, **long**s are 8—so a C# sender and receiver only need to agree on the primitive type to be used. (Communicating with a non-C# application may be more complex.) The size of an integer type, along with the encoding (signed/unsigned, see below), determines the maximum and minimum values that can be represented using that type.

- *Byte order:* Are the bytes of the binary representation written to the stream (or placed in the byte array) from left to right or right to left? If the most significant byte is transmitted first and the least significant byte is transmitted last, that's the so-called big-endian order. Little-endian is, of course, just the opposite.

- *Signed or unsigned:* Signed integers are usually transmitted in *two's-complement* representation. For k-bit numbers, the two's-complement encoding of the negative integer $-n$, $1 \le n \le 2^{k-1}$, is the binary value of $2^k - n$; and the nonnegative integer p, $0 \le p \le 2^{k-1} - 1$, is encoded simply by the k-bit binary value of p. Thus, given k

bits, two's complement can represent values in the range -2^{k-1} through $2^{k-1} - 1$, and the most significant bit (msb) tells whether the value is positive (msb = 0) or negative (msb = 1). On the other hand, a k-bit *unsigned* integer can encode values in the range 0 through $2^k - 1$ directly.

Consider again the *itemNumber*. It is a **long**, so its binary representation is 64 bits (8 bytes). If its value is 12345654321 and the encoding is big-endian, the 8 bytes sent would be (with the byte on the left transmitted first):

0	0	0	2	223	219	188	49

If, on the other hand, the value was sent in little-endian order, the transmitted byte values would be:

49	188	219	223	2	0	0	0

If the sender uses big-endian when the receiver is expecting little-endian, the receiver will end up with an *itemNumber* of 3583981154337816576! Most network protocols specify big-endian byte order; in fact it is sometimes called *network byte order*. However, Intel-, AMD-, and Alpha-based architectures (which are the primary architectures used by the Microsoft Windows operating system) are by default little-endian order. If your program will only be communicating with other C# programs on Windows operating systems, this may not a problem. However, if you are communicating with a program using another hardware architecture, or written in another language (e.g., Java, which uses big-endian byte order by default), byte order can become an issue. For this reason, it is always good form to convert outgoing multibyte binary numbers to big-endian, and incoming multibyte binary numbers from big-endian to "local" format. This conversion capability is provided in the .NET framework by both the IPAddress class static methods NetworkToHostOrder() and HostToNetworkOrder(), and constructor options in the UnicodeEncoding class.

Note that the most significant bit of the 64-bit binary value of 12345654321 is 0, so its signed (two's-complement) and unsigned representations are the same. More generally, the distinction between k-bit signed and unsigned values is irrelevant for values that lie in the range 0 through $2^{k-1} - 1$. However, protocols often use unsigned integers; C# does provide support for unsigned integers, however, that support is not considered CLR (Common Language Runtime) compliant. The .NET CLR was designed to provide language portability, and therefore is restricted to using the least common denominator of its supported languages, which does not include unsigned types. There is no immediate drawback to using the non-CLR compliant unsigned types, other than possible cross-language integration issues (particularly with Java/J++, which do not define unsigned numbers as base types).

As with strings, .NET provides mechanisms to turn primitive integer types into sequences of bytes and vice versa. In particular, the BinaryWriter class has a Write()

method that is overloaded to accept different type arguments, including short, int, and long. These methods allow those types to be written out directly in two's-complement representation (explicit encoding needs to be specified in the BinaryWriter constructor or manual conversion methods need to be invoked to convert the values to big-endian). Similarly, the BinaryReader class has methods ReadInt32() (for int), ReadInt16() (for short) and ReadInt64() (for long). The next section describes some ways to compose instances of these classes.

3.2 Composing I/O Streams

The .NET framework's stream classes can be composed to provide powerful encoding and decoding facilities. For example, we can wrap the NetworkStream of a TcpClient instance in a BufferedStream instance to improve performance by buffering bytes temporarily and flushing them to the underlying channel all at once. We can then wrap that instance in a BinaryWriter to send primitive data types. We would code this composition as follows:

```
TcpClient client = new TcpClient(server, port);
BinaryWriter out = new BinaryWriter(new BufferedStream(client.GetStream()));
```

Figure 3.1 demonstrates this composition. Here, we write our primitive data values, one by one, to BinaryWriter, which writes the binary data to BufferedStream, which buffers the data from the three writes, and then writes once to the socket NetworkStream, which controls writing to the network. We create a identical composition with a BinaryReader on the other endpoint to efficiently receive primitive data types.

A complete description of the .NET I/O API is beyond the scope of this text; however, Table 3.1 provides a list of some of the relevant .NET I/O classes as a starting point for exploiting its capabilities.

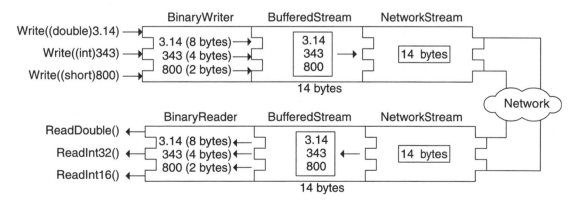

Figure 3.1: Stream composition.

I/O Class	Function
BufferedStream	Performs buffering for I/O optimization.
BinaryReader/BinaryWriter	Handles read/write for primitive data types.
MemoryStream	Creates streams that have memory as a backing store, and can be used in place of temporary buffers and files.
Stream	Abstract base class of all streams.
StreamReader/StreamWriter	Read and write character input/output to/from a stream in a specified encoding.
StringReader/StringWriter	Read and write character input/output to/from a string in a specified encoding.
TextReader/TextWriter	Abstract base class for reading and writing character input/output. Base class of StreamReader/Writer and StringReader/Writer.

Table 3.1: .NET I/O Classes

3.3 Framing and Parsing

Converting data to wire format is, of course, only half the story; the original information must be recovered at the receiver from the transmitted sequence of bytes. Application protocols typically deal with discrete messages, which are viewed as collections of fields. *Framing* refers to the problem of enabling the receiver to locate the beginning and end of the message in the stream and of the fields within the message. Whether information is encoded as text, as multibyte binary numbers, or as some combination of the two, the application protocol must enable the receiver of a message to determine when it has received all of the message and to parse it into fields.

If the fields in a message all have fixed sizes and the message is made up of a fixed number of fields, then the size of the message is known in advance and the receiver can simply read the expected number of bytes into a **byte**[] buffer. This technique was used in TCPEchoClient.cs, where we knew the number of bytes to expect from the server. However, when some field (and/or the whole message) can vary in length, as with the *itemDescription* in our example, we do not know beforehand how many bytes to read.

Marking the end of the message is easy in the special case of the last message to be sent on a TCP connection: the sender simply closes the sending side of the connection (using Shutdown(SocketShutdown.Send)[1] or Close()) after sending the message. After the receiver reads the last byte of the message, it receives an end-of-stream indication (i.e., Read() returns 0), and thus can tell that it has as much of the message as there will ever be. The same principle applies to the last field in a message sent as a UDP datagram packet.

---

[1] The Shutdown() method is only available in .NET in the Socket class. See Section 4.6 for a mechanism to utilize this functionality for .NET's higher level socket classes as well.

In all other cases, the message itself must contain additional framing information enabling the receiver to parse the field/message. This information typically takes one of the following forms:

- *Delimiter*: The end of the variable-length field or message is indicated by a *unique marker*, an explicit byte sequence that immediately follows, but does not occur in, the data.

- *Explicit length*: The variable-length field or message is preceded by a (fixed-size) length field that tells how many bytes it contains.

The delimiter-based approach is often used with variable-length text: A particular character or sequence of characters is defined to mark the end of the field. If the entire message consists of text, it is straightforward to read in characters using an instance of a TextReader (which handles the byte-to-character translation), looking for the delimiter sequence, and returning the character string preceding it.

Unfortunately, the TextReader classes do not support reading binary data. Moreover, the relationship between the number of *bytes* read from the underlying NetworkStream and the number of *characters* read from the TextReader is unspecified, especially with multibyte encodings. When a message uses a combination of the two framing methods mentioned above, with some explicit-length-delimited fields and others using character markers, this can create problems.

The class Framer, defined below, allows NetworkStream to be parsed as a sequence of fields delimited by specific byte patterns. The static method Framer.nextToken() reads bytes from the given Stream until it encounters the given sequence of bytes or the stream ends. All bytes read up to that point are then returned in a new byte array. If the end of the stream is encountered before any data is read, null is returned. The delimiter can be different for each call to nextToken(), and the method is completely independent of any encoding.

A couple of words of caution are in order here. First, nextToken() is terribly inefficient; for real applications, a more efficient pattern-matching algorithm should be used. Second, when using Framer.nextToken() with text-based message formats, the caller must convert the delimiter from a character string to a byte array and the returned byte array to a character string. In this case the character encoding needs to distribute over concatenation, so that it doesn't matter whether a string is converted to bytes all at once or a little bit at a time.

To make this precise, let $E()$ represent an encoding—that is, a function that maps character sequences to byte sequences. Let a and b be sequences of characters, so $E(a)$ denotes the sequence of bytes that is the result of encoding a. Let "+" denote concatenation of sequences, so $a + b$ is the sequence consisting of a followed by b. This explicit-conversion approach (as opposed to parsing the message as a character stream) should only be used with encodings that have the property that $E(a + b) = E(a) + E(b)$; otherwise, the results may be unexpected. Although most encodings supported in .NET have this property, some do not. In particular, the big- and little-endian versions of Unicode encode a String by first outputting a byte-order indicator (the 2-byte sequence 254–255 for big-endian, and 255–254 for little-endian), followed by the 16-bit Unicode value of each character in the String, in the indicated byte order. Thus, the encoding of "Big fox" using big-endian Unicode with a byte-order marker is as follows:

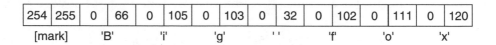

254	255	0	66	0	105	0	103	0	32	0	102	0	111	0	120
[mark]		'B'		'i'		'g'		' '		'f'		'o'		'x'	

The encoding, on the other hand, of "Big" concatenated with the encoding of "fox," using the same encoding, is as follows:

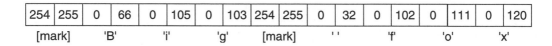

254	255	0	66	0	105	0	103	254	255	0	32	0	102	0	111	0	120
[mark]		'B'		'i'		'g'		[mark]		' '		'f'		'o'		'x'	

Using either of these encodings to convert the delimiter results in a byte sequence that begins with the byte-order marker. The encodings BigEndianUnicode and Unicode (little-endian) omit the byte-order marker, and the UnicodeEncoding class omits it unless specified otherwise in the constructor, so they are suitable for use with Framer. nextToken().

Framer.cs

```
0   using System;      // For Boolean
1   using System.IO;   // For Stream
2
3   public class Framer {
4
5     public static byte[] nextToken(Stream input, byte[] delimiter) {
6       int nextByte;
7
8       // If the stream has already ended, return null
9       if ((nextByte = input.ReadByte()) == -1)
10        return null;
11
12      MemoryStream tokenBuffer = new MemoryStream();
13      do {
14        tokenBuffer.WriteByte((byte)nextByte);
15        byte[] currentToken = tokenBuffer.ToArray();
16        if (endsWith(currentToken, delimiter)) {
```

```
17           int tokenLength = currentToken.Length - delimiter.Length;
18           byte[] token = new byte[tokenLength];
19           Array.Copy(currentToken, 0, token, 0, tokenLength);
20            return token;
21          }
22      } while ((nextByte = input.ReadByte()) != -1);   // Stop on EOS
23      return tokenBuffer.ToArray();              // Received at least one byte
24    }
25
26    // Returns true if value ends with the bytes in the suffix
27    private static Boolean endsWith(byte[] value, byte[] suffix) {
28      if (value.Length < suffix.Length)
29        return false;
30
31      for (int offset=1; offset <= suffix.Length; offset++)
32        if (value[value.Length - offset] != suffix[suffix.Length - offset])
33          return false;
34
35      return true;
36    }
37  }
```

Framer.cs

1. nextToken(): lines 5–24
   Read from input stream until delimiter or end-of-stream.
   - **Test for end-of-stream:** lines 8–10
     If the input stream is already at end-of-stream, return null.
   - **Create a buffer to hold the bytes of the token:** line 12
     We use a MemoryStream to collect the data byte by byte. The MemoryStream class allows a byte array to be handled like a stream of bytes.
   - **Put the last byte read into the buffer:** line 14
   - **Get a byte array containing the input so far:** line 15
     It is very inefficient to create a new byte array on each iteration, but it is simple.
   - **Check whether the delimiter is a suffix of the current token:** lines 16–21
     If so, create a new byte array containing the bytes read so far, minus the delimiter suffix, and return it.
   - **Get next byte:** line 22
   - **Return the current token on end-of-stream:** line 23

2. endsWith(): lines 26–36
   - **Compare lengths:** lines 28–29
     The candidate sequence must be at least as long as the delimiter to be a match.
   - **Compare bytes, return** false **on any difference:** lines 31–33
     Compare the last *suffix.Length* bytes of the token to the delimiter.
   - **If no difference, return** true: line 35

3.4 Implementing Wire Formats in C#

To emphasize the fact that the same information can be represented "on the wire" in different ways, we define an interface ItemQuoteEncoder, which has a single method that takes an ItemQuote instance and converts it to a **byte**[] that can be written to a NetworkStream or sent as is for datagrams or direct Sockets.

ItemQuoteEncoder.cs

```
0  public interface ItemQuoteEncoder {
1    byte[] encode(ItemQuote item);
2  }
```

ItemQuoteEncoder.cs

The specification of the corresponding decoding functionality is given by the ItemQuoteDecoder interface, which has methods for parsing messages received via streams or in byte arrays used for UDP packets. Each method performs the same function: extracting the information for one message and returning an ItemQuote instance containing the information.

ItemQuoteDecoder.cs

```
0  using System.IO; // For Stream
1
2  public interface ItemQuoteDecoder {
3    ItemQuote decode(Stream source);
4    ItemQuote decode(byte[] packet);
5  }
```

ItemQuoteDecoder.cs

Sections 3.4.1 and 3.4.2 present two different implementations for these interfaces: one using a text representation, the other, a hybrid encoding.

3.4.1   Text-Oriented Representation

Clearly we can represent the ItemQuote information as text. One possibility is simply to transmit the output of the ToString() method using a suitable character encoding. To simplify parsing, the approach in this section uses a different representation, in which the values of *itemNumber*, *itemDescription*, and so on are transmitted as a sequence of delimited text fields. The sequence of fields is as follows:

⟨Item Number⟩ ⟨Description⟩ ⟨Quantity⟩ ⟨Price⟩ ⟨Discount?⟩ ⟨In Stock?⟩

The Item Number field (and the other integer-valued fields, Quantity and Price) contain a sequence of decimal-digit characters followed by a space character (the delimiter). The Description field is just the description text. However, because the text itself may include the space character, we have to use a different delimiter; we choose the newline character, represented as \n in C#, as the delimiter for this field.

Boolean values can be encoded in several different ways. Although a single-byte Boolean is one of the overloaded arguments in the BinaryWriter Write() method, in order to keep our wire format slightly more language agnostic (and to allow it to communicate with the Java versions of these programs [25]) we opted not to use it. Another possibility is to include the string "true" or the string "false," according to the value of the variable. A more compact approach (and the one used here) is to encode both values (*discounted* and *inStock*) in a single field; the field contains the character 'd' if *discounted* is true, indicating that the item is discounted, and the character 's' if *inStock* is true, indicating that the item is in stock. The absence of a character indicates that the corresponding Boolean is false, so this field may be empty. Again, a different delimiter (\n) is used for this final field, to make it slightly easier to recognize the end of the message even when this field is empty. A quote for 23 units of item number 12345, which has the description "AAA Battery" and a price of $14.45, and which is both in stock and discounted, would be represented as

12345 AAA Battery\n23 1445 ds\n

Constants needed by both the encoder and the decoder are defined in the ItemQuote-TextConst interface, which defines "ascii" as the default encoding (we could just as easily have used any other encoding as the default) and 1024 as the maximum length (in bytes) of an encoded message. Limiting the length of an encoded message limits the flexibility of the protocol, but it also provides for sanity checks by the receiver.

ItemQuoteTextConst.cs

```
0   using System; // For String
1
2   public class ItemQuoteTextConst {
3     public static readonly String DEFAULT_CHAR_ENC = "ascii";
4     public static readonly int MAX_WIRE_LENGTH = 1024;
5   }
```

ItemQuoteEncoderText implements the text encoding.

ItemQuoteEncoderText.cs

```
0  using System;       // For String, Activator
1  using System.IO;    // For IOException
2  using System.Text;  // For Encoding
3
4  public class ItemQuoteEncoderText : ItemQuoteEncoder {
5
6    public Encoding encoding; // Character encoding
7
8    public ItemQuoteEncoderText() : this(ItemQuoteTextConst.DEFAULT_CHAR_ENC) {
9    }
10
11   public ItemQuoteEncoderText(string encodingDesc) {
12     encoding = Encoding.GetEncoding(encodingDesc);
13   }
14
15   public byte[] encode(ItemQuote item) {
16
17     String EncodedString = item.itemNumber + " ";
18     if (item.itemDescription.IndexOf('\n') != -1)
19       throw new IOException("Invalid description (contains newline)");
20     EncodedString = EncodedString + item.itemDescription + "\n";
21     EncodedString = EncodedString + item.quantity + " ";
22     EncodedString = EncodedString + item.unitPrice + " ";
23
24     if (item.discounted)
25       EncodedString = EncodedString + "d"; // Only include 'd' if discounted
26     if (item.inStock)
27       EncodedString = EncodedString + "s"; // Only include 's' if in stock
28     EncodedString = EncodedString + "\n";
29
30     if (EncodedString.Length > ItemQuoteTextConst.MAX_WIRE_LENGTH)
31       throw new IOException("Encoded length too long");
32
33     byte[] buf = encoding.GetBytes(EncodedString);
34
```

```
35      return buf;
36
37    }
38  }
```

1. **Constructors:** lines 8–13
   If no encoding is explicitly specified, we use the default encoding specified in the constant interface. The Encoding class method GetEncoding() takes a string argument that specifies the encoding to use, in this case the default is the constant "ascii" from ItemQuoteTextConst.cs.

2. encode() **method:** lines 15–37
   - **Write the first integer, followed by a space delimiter:** line 17
   - **Check for delimiter:** lines 18–19
     Make sure that the field delimiter is not contained in the field itself. If it is, throw an exception.
   - **Output** *itemDescription* **and other integers:** lines 20–22
   - **Write the flag characters if the Booleans are true:** lines 24–27
   - **Write the delimiter for the flag field:** line 28
   - **Validate that the encoded length is within the maximum size limit:** lines 30–31
   - **Convert the encoded string from the given encoding to a byte array:** line 33
   - **Return the byte array:** line 35

The decoding class ItemQuoteDecoderText simply inverts the encoding process.

ItemQuoteDecoderText.cs

```
0  using System;       // For String, Activator
1  using System.Text;  // For Encoding
2  using System.IO;    // For Stream
3
4  public class ItemQuoteDecoderText : ItemQuoteDecoder {
5
6    public Encoding encoding; // Character encoding
7
8    public ItemQuoteDecoderText() : this (ItemQuoteTextConst.DEFAULT_CHAR_ENC) {
9    }
```

```
10
11    public ItemQuoteDecoderText(String encodingDesc) {
12      encoding = Encoding.GetEncoding(encodingDesc);
13    }
14
15    public ItemQuote decode(Stream wire) {
16      String itemNo, description, quant, price, flags;
17
18      byte[] space = encoding.GetBytes(" ");
19      byte[] newline = encoding.GetBytes("\n");
20
21      itemNo = encoding.GetString(Framer.nextToken(wire, space));
22      description = encoding.GetString(Framer.nextToken(wire, newline));
23      quant = encoding.GetString(Framer.nextToken(wire, space));
24      price = encoding.GetString(Framer.nextToken(wire, space));
25      flags = encoding.GetString(Framer.nextToken(wire, newline));
26
27      return new ItemQuote(Int64.Parse(itemNo), description,
28                           Int32.Parse(quant),
29                           Int32.Parse(price),
30                           (flags.IndexOf('d') != -1),
31                           (flags.IndexOf('s') != -1));
32    }
33
34    public ItemQuote decode(byte[] packet) {
35      Stream payload = new MemoryStream(packet, 0, packet.Length, false);
36      return decode(payload);
37    }
38  }
```

ItemQuoteDecoderText.cs

1. **Variables and constructors:** lines 6–13
   - **Encoding:** line 6
     The encoding used in the decoder must be the same as in the encoder!
   - **Constructors:** lines 8–13
     If no encoding is given at construction time, the default defined in ItemQuote-TextConst is used.

2. **Stream** decode(): lines 15–32
   - **Convert delimiters:** lines 18–19
     We get the encoded form of the delimiters ahead of time, for efficiency.

- **Call the** nextToken() **method for each field:** lines 21–25
  For each field, we call Framer.nextToken() with the appropriate delimiter and convert the result according to the specified encoding.
- **Construct** ItemQuote: lines 27–31
  Convert to native types using the wrapper conversion methods and test for the presence of the flag characters in the last field.

3. **Byte array** decode(): lines 34–37
   For UDP packets, convert the byte array to a stream, and then call the stream decode() method.

3.4.2 Combined Data Representation

Our next encoding represents the integers of the ItemQuote as fixed-size, binary numbers: *itemNumber* as 64 bits, and *quantity* and *unitPrice* as 32 bits. It encodes the Boolean values as flag bits, which occupy the smallest possible space in an encoded message. Also, the variable-length string *itemDescription* is encoded in a field with an explicit length indication. The binary encoding and decoding share coding constants in the ItemQuoteBinConst interface.

ItemQuoteBinConst.cs

```
0  using System; // For String
1
2  public class ItemQuoteBinConst {
3    public static readonly String DEFAULT_CHAR_ENC = "ascii";
4
5    public static readonly byte DISCOUNT_FLAG = 1 << 7;
6    public static readonly byte IN_STOCK_FLAG = 1 << 0;
7    public static readonly int MAX_DESC_LEN = 255;
8    public static readonly int MAX_WIRE_LENGTH = 1024;
9  }
```

ItemQuoteBinConst.cs

ItemQuoteEncoderBin implements the binary encoding.

ItemQuoteEncoderBin.cs

```
0  using System;          // For String, Activator
1  using System.IO;       // For BinaryWriter
2  using System.Text;     // For Encoding
3  using System.Net;      // For IPAddress
```

```
 4
 5   public class ItemQuoteEncoderBin : ItemQuoteEncoder {
 6
 7     public Encoding encoding; // Character encoding
 8
 9     public ItemQuoteEncoderBin() : this (ItemQuoteBinConst.DEFAULT_CHAR_ENC) {
10     }
11
12     public ItemQuoteEncoderBin(String encodingDesc) {
13       encoding = Encoding.GetEncoding(encodingDesc);
14     }
15
16     public byte[] encode(ItemQuote item) {
17
18       MemoryStream mem = new MemoryStream();
19       BinaryWriter output = new BinaryWriter(new BufferedStream(mem));
20
21       output.Write(IPAddress.HostToNetworkOrder(item.itemNumber));
22       output.Write(IPAddress.HostToNetworkOrder(item.quantity));
23       output.Write(IPAddress.HostToNetworkOrder(item.unitPrice));
24
25       byte flags = 0;
26       if (item.discounted)
27         flags |= ItemQuoteBinConst.DISCOUNT_FLAG;
28       if (item.inStock)
29         flags |= ItemQuoteBinConst.IN_STOCK_FLAG;
30       output.Write(flags);
31
32       byte[] encodedDesc = encoding.GetBytes(item.itemDescription);
33       if (encodedDesc.Length > ItemQuoteBinConst.MAX_DESC_LEN)
34         throw new IOException("Item Description exceeds encoded length limit");
35       output.Write((byte)encodedDesc.Length);
36       output.Write(encodedDesc);
37
38       output.Flush();
39
40       return mem.ToArray();
41     }
42   }
```

ItemQuoteEncoderBin.cs

1. **Constants, variables, and constructors:** lines 7–14
2. encode(): lines 16–41
   - **Set up Output:** lines 18–19
     A MemoryStream collects the bytes of the encoded message. Encapsulating the MemoryStream in a BinaryWriter allows the use of its methods for writing binary integers.
   - **Write integers:** lines 21–23
     The Write() method is overloaded to write all of the basic C# data types. The static IPAddress.HostToNetworkOrder() method converts each integer to big-endian order, and is also overloaded to accept **long**s, **int**s, and **short**s, and returns the same size integer as it was passed.
   - **Write Booleans as flags:** lines 25–30
     Encode each Boolean using a single bit in a flag byte. Initialize the flag byte to 0, then set the appropriate bits to 1, if either *discounted* or *inStock* is true. (The bits are defined in the ItemQuoteBinConst interface to be the most and least significant bits of the byte, respectively.) Write the byte to the stream.
   - **Convert description string to bytes:** line 32
     Convert the text to bytes in the specified encoding.
   - **Check description length:** lines 33–34
     We are going to use an explicit length encoding for the string, with a single byte giving the length. The biggest value that byte can contain is 255 bytes, so the length of the encoded string must not exceed 255 bytes. If it does, we throw an exception.
   - **Write encoded string:** lines 35–36
     Write the length of the encoded string, followed by the bytes in the buffer.
   - **Flush output stream, return bytes:** line 38
     Ensure that all bytes are flushed from the MemoryStream to the underlying byte buffer.
   - **Return the byte array to be sent:** line 40

ItemQuoteDecoderBin implements the corresponding decoder function.

ItemQuoteDecoderBin.cs

```
0  using System;          // For String, Activator
1  using System.IO;       // For Stream
2  using System.Text;     // For Encoding
3  using System.Net;      // For IPAddress
4
5  public class ItemQuoteDecoderBin : ItemQuoteDecoder {
6
```

```
7    public Encoding encoding; // Character encoding
8
9    public ItemQuoteDecoderBin() : this (ItemQuoteTextConst.DEFAULT_CHAR_ENC) {
10   }
11
12   public ItemQuoteDecoderBin(String encodingDesc) {
13     encoding = Encoding.GetEncoding(encodingDesc);
14   }
15
16   public ItemQuote decode(Stream wire) {
17     BinaryReader src = new BinaryReader(new BufferedStream(wire));
18
19     long itemNumber = IPAddress.NetworkToHostOrder(src.ReadInt64());
20     int quantity = IPAddress.NetworkToHostOrder(src.ReadInt32());
21     int unitPrice = IPAddress.NetworkToHostOrder(src.ReadInt32());
22     byte flags = src.ReadByte();
23
24     int stringLength = src.Read(); // Returns an unsigned byte as an int
25     if (stringLength == -1)
26       throw new EndOfStreamException();
27     byte[] stringBuf = new byte[stringLength];
28     src.Read(stringBuf, 0, stringLength);
29     String itemDesc = encoding.GetString(stringBuf);
30
31     return new ItemQuote(itemNumber,itemDesc, quantity, unitPrice,
32       ((flags & ItemQuoteBinConst.DISCOUNT_FLAG) == ItemQuoteBinConst.DISCOUNT_FLAG),
33       ((flags & ItemQuoteBinConst.IN_STOCK_FLAG) == ItemQuoteBinConst.IN_STOCK_FLAG));
34   }
35
36   public ItemQuote decode(byte[] packet) {
37     Stream payload = new MemoryStream(packet, 0, packet.Length, false);
38     return decode(payload);
39   }
40 }
```

ItemQuoteDecoderBin.cs

1. **Constants, variables, and constructors:** lines 7–14

2. **Stream decode:** lines 16–34

- **Wrap the input** Stream: line 17
  Using the given Stream, construct a BinaryReader so we can make use of the methods readInt64(), readInt32(), and readByte() for reading binary data types from the input.

- **Read integers:** lines 19–21
  Read the integers back in the same order in which they were written out. The readInt64() method reads 8 bytes (64 bits) and constructs a (signed) **long**. The readInt32() method reads 4 bytes and constructs a (signed) **int**. The static method IPAddress.NetworkToHostOrder() converts from big-endian (network) byte ordering to the host's native byte ordering; if the native ordering is big-endian, the data is returned unmodified. Either will throw an EndOfStreamException if the stream ends before the requisite number of bytes is read.

- **Read flag byte:** line 22
  The flag byte is next; the values of the individual bits will be checked later.

- **Read string length:** lines 24–26
  The next byte contains the length of the encoded string. Note that we use the Read() method, which returns the contents of the next byte read as an integer between 0 and 255, and that we read it into an **int**.

- **Allocate buffer and read encoded string:** lines 27–29
  Once we know how long the encoded string is, we allocate a buffer and call Read() specifying the expected number of bytes. Read() will throw an EndOfStream-Exception if the stream ends before the buffer is filled. Note the advantage of the length-prefixed String representation: bytes do not have to be interpreted as characters until you have them all.

- **Check flags:** lines 32–33
  The expressions used as parameters in the call to the constructor illustrate the standard method of checking whether a particular bit is set (equal to 1) in an integer type.

3. **Byte array decode:** lines 36–39
   Simply wrap the packet's byte array in a MemoryStream and pass to the stream-decoding method.

3.4.3 Sending and Receiving

The encodings presented above can be used with both the NetworkStreams of .NET's TcpClient and TcpListener, and with the byte arrays of the UdpClient class. We show the TCP usage first.

SendTcp.cs

```
0  using System;               // For String, Console, ArgumentException
1  using System.Net.Sockets;   // For TcpClient, NetworkStream
2
```

```
3  class SendTcp {
4
5    static void Main(string[] args) {
6
7      if (args.Length != 2) // Test for correct # of args
8        throw new ArgumentException("Parameters: <Destination> <Port>");
9
10     String server = args[0];              // Destination address
11     int servPort = Int32.Parse(args[1]); // Destination port
12
13     // Create socket that is connected to server on specified port
14     TcpClient client = new TcpClient(server, servPort);
15     NetworkStream netStream = client.GetStream();
16
17     ItemQuote quote = new ItemQuote(1234567890987654L, "5mm Super Widgets",
18                                    1000, 12999, true, false);
19
20     // Send text-encoded quote
21     ItemQuoteEncoderText coder = new ItemQuoteEncoderText();
22     byte[] codedQuote = coder.encode(quote);
23     Console.WriteLine("Sending Text-Encoded Quote (" +
24                       codedQuote.Length + " bytes): ");
25     Console.WriteLine(quote);
26
27     netStream.Write(codedQuote, 0, codedQuote.Length);
28
29     // Receive binary-encoded quote
30     ItemQuoteDecoder decoder = new ItemQuoteDecoderBin();
31     ItemQuote receivedQuote = decoder.decode(client.GetStream());
32     Console.WriteLine("Received Binary-Encode Quote:");
33     Console.WriteLine(receivedQuote);
34
35     netStream.Close();
36     client.Close();
37   }
38 }
```

SendTcp.cs

1. TcpClient **setup:** lines 13–15
2. **Send using text encoding:** lines 20–27
3. **Receive using binary encoding:** lines 29–33

RecvTcp.cs

```
0   using System;                // For Console, Int32, ArgumentException
1   using System.Net;            // For IPAddress
2   using System.Net.Sockets;    // For TcpListener, TcpClient
3
4   class RecvTcp {
5
6     static void Main(string[] args) {
7
8       if (args.Length != 1) // Test for correct # of args
9         throw new ArgumentException("Parameters: <Port>");
10
11      int port = Int32.Parse(args[0]);
12
13      // Create a TCPListener to accept client connections
14      TcpListener listener = new TcpListener(IPAddress.Any, port);
15      listener.Start();
16
17      TcpClient client = listener.AcceptTcpClient(); // Get client connection
18
19      // Receive text-encoded quote
20      ItemQuoteDecoder decoder = new ItemQuoteDecoderText();
21      ItemQuote quote = decoder.decode(client.GetStream());
22      Console.WriteLine("Received Text-Encoded Quote:");
23      Console.WriteLine(quote);
24
25      // Repeat quote with binary-encoding, adding 10 cents to the price
26      ItemQuoteEncoder encoder = new ItemQuoteEncoderBin();
27      quote.unitPrice += 10; // Add 10 cents to unit price
28      Console.WriteLine("Sending (binary)...");
29      byte[] bytesToSend = encoder.encode(quote);
30      client.GetStream().Write(bytesToSend, 0, bytesToSend.Length);
31
32      client.Close();
33      listener.Stop();
34    }
35  }
```

RecvTcp.cs

1. TcpListener **setup:** lines 13–15
2. **Accept client connection:** line 17

3. **Receive and print out a text-encoded message:** lines 19–23

4. **Send a binary-encoded message:** lines 25–30
   Note that before sending, we add 10 cents to the unit price given in the original message.

To demonstrate the use of the encoding and decoding classes with datagrams, we include a simple UDP sender and receiver. Since this is very similar to the TCP code, we do not include any code description.

SendUdp.cs

```
0   using System;              // For String, Int32, ArgumentException
1   using System.Net.Sockets;  // For UdpClient
2
3   class SendUdp {
4
5     static void Main(string[] args) {
6
7       if (args.Length != 2 && args.Length != 3)  // Test for correct # of args
8         throw new ArgumentException("Parameter(s): <Destination>" +
9                                      " <Port> [<encoding]");
10
11      String server = args[0];            // Server name or IP address
12      int destPort = Int32.Parse(args[1]); // Destination port
13
14      ItemQuote quote = new ItemQuote(1234567890987654L, "5mm Super Widgets",
15                                      1000, 12999, true, false);
16
17      UdpClient client = new UdpClient(); // UDP socket for sending
18
19      ItemQuoteEncoder encoder = (args.Length == 3 ?
20                                  new ItemQuoteEncoderText(args[2]) :
21                                  new ItemQuoteEncoderText());
22
23      byte[] codedQuote = encoder.encode(quote);
24
25      client.Send(codedQuote, codedQuote.Length, server, destPort);
26
27      client.Close();
28    }
29  }
```

RecvUdp.cs

```
0  using System;             // For Int32, ArgumentException
1  using System.Net;         // For IPEndPoint
2  using System.Net.Sockets; // For UdpClient
3
4  class RecvUdp {
5
6    static void Main(string[] args) {
7
8      if (args.Length != 1 && args.Length != 2)  // Test for correct # of args
9        throw new ArgumentException("Parameter(s): <Port> [<encoding>]");
10
11     int port = Int32.Parse(args[0]);   // Receiving Port
12
13     UdpClient client = new UdpClient(port); // UDP socket for receiving
14
15     byte[] packet = new byte[ItemQuoteTextConst.MAX_WIRE_LENGTH];
16     IPEndPoint remoteIPEndPoint = new IPEndPoint(IPAddress.Any, port);
17
18     packet = client.Receive(ref remoteIPEndPoint);
19
20     ItemQuoteDecoderText decoder = (args.Length == 2 ?   // Which encoding
21                                    new ItemQuoteDecoderText(args[1]) :
22                                    new ItemQuoteDecoderText() );
23
24     ItemQuote quote = decoder.decode(packet);
25     Console.WriteLine(quote);
26
27     client.Close();
28   }
29 }
```

RecvUdp.cs

3.5 Wrapping Up

We have seen how C# data types can be encoded in different ways and how messages can be constructed from various types of information. You may be aware that the .NET framework includes *serialization* capabilities: The System.Xml.Serializable and

System.Runtime.Serialization.Formatters name spaces contain classes that support writing a C# class instance to an XML (eXtensible Markup Language) file, binary format, or SOAP (Simple Object Access Protocol) message suitable for sending over a network connection. Once at the remote host, the file can be deserialized into a instance of that object. Similarly, the System.Runtime.Remoting name space allows the ability to create a remote proxy object that a client can use to invoke methods on a server's object. It might seem that having these interfaces available would eliminate the need for what we have described in this chapter, and that is true to some extent. However, it is not always the case for several reasons.

First, the encoded forms produced by Serializable may not be very efficient. They may include information that is meaningless outside the context of the Common Language Runtime (CLR), and may also incur overhead to provide flexibility that may not be needed. Second, Serializable and Remoting cannot be used when a different wire format has already been specified—for example, by a standardized protocol. And finally, custom-designed classes have to provide their own implementations of the serialization interfaces anyway.

A basic tenet of good protocol design is that the protocol should constrain the implementor as little as possible and should minimize assumptions about the platform on which the protocol will be implemented. We therefore avoid the use of Serializable and Remoting in this book, and instead use more direct encoding and decoding methods.

3.6 Exercises

1. What happens if the Encoder uses a different encoding than the Decoder?

2. Rewrite the binary encoder so that the Item Description is terminated by "\r\n" instead of being length encoded. Use Send/RecvTcp to test this new encoding.

3. The nextToken() method of Framer assumes that either the delimiter or an end-of-stream (EoS) terminates a token; however, finding the EoS may be an error in some protocols. Rewrite nextToken() to include a second Boolean parameter. If the parameter value is true, then the EoS terminates a token without error; otherwise, the EoS generates an error.

4. Using the code provided on the website of the Java version of this book ([25], *www.mkp.com/practical/javasockets*), run a C# receiver and a Java sender, and vice versa. Verify that the contents are sent and received properly. Try removing the NetworkToHostOrdering() and HostToNetworkOrdering() method calls and rerunning the experiment.

chapter **4**

Beyond the Basics

The client and server examples in Chapter 2 demonstrate the basic model for programming with sockets in C#. The next step is to apply these concepts in various programming models, such as nonblocking I/O, threading, asynchronous I/O, and multicasting.

4.1 Nonblocking I/O

Socket I/O calls may block for several reasons. Data input methods Read(), Receive(), and ReceiveFrom() block if data is not available. Data output methods Write(), Send(), or SendTo() may block if there is not sufficient space to buffer the transmitted data. The Accept(), AcceptSocket(), and AcceptTcpClient() methods of the Socket and TcpListener classes all block until a connection has been established (see Section 5.4). Meanwhile, long round-trip times, high error rate connections, and slow (or deceased) servers may cause connection establishment to take a long time. In all of these cases, the method returns only after the request has been satisfied. Of course, a blocking method call halts the execution of the application. And we have not even considered the possibility of a buggy or malicious application on the other end of the connection!

What about a program that has other tasks to perform while waiting for call completion (e.g., updating the "busy" cursor or responding to user requests)? These programs may have no time to wait on a blocked method call. Or what about lost UDP datagrams? Fortunately, several mechanisms are available for avoiding unwanted blocking behaviors. We deal with three here: (1) I/O status prechecking, (2) blocking timeout calls, and (3) nonblocking sockets. Table 4.1 summarizes the techniques according to the type of socket you are using. Later, we'll look at a fourth method, called asynchronous I/O, where instead

I/O Operation	Socket Type	Blocking Avoidance Options
Accepting a new connection	Socket	1. Set the socket to nonblocking before calling Accept(). 2. Call Poll() or Select() on the socket before calling Accept().
	TcpListener	1. Only call AcceptSocket() or AcceptTcpClient() if Pending() returns true.
Making a new connection	Socket	1. Set the socket to nonblocking before calling Connect(). 2. Call Poll() or Select() on the socket before calling Connect().
Send	Socket	1. Set the socket to nonblocking before calling Send() or SendTo(). 2. Call Poll() or Select() on the socket before calling Send() or SendTo(). 3. Set the SendTimeout socket option before calling Send() or SendTo().
	TcpClient	1. Set the SendTimeout property before calling Write() on the network stream.
Receive	Socket	1. Set the socket to nonblocking before calling Receive() or ReceiveFrom(). 2. Call Poll() or Select() on the socket before calling Receive() or ReceiveFrom(). 3. Set the ReceiveTimeout socket option before calling Receive() or ReceiveFrom(). 4. Only call Receive() or ReceiveFrom() if property Available > 0.
	TcpClient	1. Set the ReceiveTimeout property before calling Read() on the network stream. 2. Only call Read() on the TcpClient's network stream if the DataAvailable property is true. (The Length property is not supported for NetworkStream.)

Table 4.1: Blocking Avoidance Mechanisms

of blocking, an I/O call immediately returns and agrees to notify you later when it has completed.

4.1.1   I/O Status Prechecking

One way to avoid blocking behavior is not to make calls that will block. How is this achieved? For some of the I/O calls that *can* block, we can precheck the I/O status to see if I/O *would* block. If the precheck indicates that the call would not block, we can proceed with the call knowing that the operation will complete immediately. If the precheck indicates that the call would block, then other processing can be done and another check can be done later.

When reading data with a TcpClient this can be achieved by checking the DataAvailable property of the associated NetworkStream, which returns true if there is data to be read and false if there is not.

```
TcpClient client = new TcpClient(server, port);
NetworkStream netstream = client.GetStream();
⋮
if (netstream.DataAvailable) {
    int len = netstream.Read(buf, 0, buf.Length);
} else {
    // No data available, do other processing
}
```

A TcpListener can precheck if there are any connections pending before calling AcceptTcpClient() or AcceptSocket() using the Pending() method. Pending() returns true if there are connections pending, false if there are not.

```
TcpListener listener = new TcpListener(ipaddr, port);
listener.Start();
⋮
if (listener.Pending()) {
    // Connections are pending, process them
    TcpClient client = listener.AcceptTcpClient();
⋮
} else {
    Console.WriteLine("No connections pending at this time.");
}
```

With the Socket class the availability of data to read can be prechecked using the Available property, which is of type int. Available always contains the number of bytes received from the network but not yet read; thus, if Available is greater than zero, a read operation will not block.

```
Socket sock = new Socket(AddressFamily.InterNetwork, SocketType.Stream,
                         ProtocolType.Tcp);
sock.Connect(serverEndPoint);
⋮
if (sock.Available > 0) {
    // We have data to read
    sock.Receive(buf, buf.Length, 0);
⋮
```

```
    } else {
        Console.WriteLine("No data available to read at this time.");
    }
```

The Poll() method of the Socket class also allows prechecking, among other features, and is discussed in the next section.

4.1.2 Blocking Calls with Timeout

In the previous section we demonstrated how to check if a call would block prior to executing it. Sometimes, however, we may actually need to know that some I/O event has *not* happened for a certain time period. For example, in Chapter 2 we saw UdpEchoClientTimeoutSocket.cs, where the client sends a datagram to the server and then waits to receive a response. If a datagram is not received before the timer expires, ReceiveFrom() unblocks to allow the client to handle the datagram loss. Utilizing socket options, the Socket class supports setting a bound on the maximum time (in milliseconds) to block on sending or receiving data, using the SocketOption.SendTimeout and SocketOption.ReceiveTimeout properties.

```
    Socket sock = new Socket(AddressFamily.InterNetwork, SocketType.Stream,
                             ProtocolType.Tcp);
    :
    sock.SetSocketOption(SocketOptionLevel.Socket,
                         SocketOptionName.SendTimeout,
                         3000); // Set a 3 second timeout on Send()/SendTo()
```

If you are using the TcpClient class, it contains the SendTimeout and ReceiveTimeout properties which can be set or retrieved.

```
    TcpClient client = new TcpClient(server, port);
    :
    client.ReceiveTimeout = 5000; // Set a 5 second timeout on Read()
```

In both cases if the specified time elapses before the method returns, a SocketException is thrown with the Socket's ErrorCode property set to 10060 (connection timed out).

The Poll() method of Socket offers more functionality. Poll() takes two options: an integer number of *microseconds* (not milliseconds) to wait for a response, and a *mode* that indicates what type of operation we are waiting for. The wait time can be negative, indicating an indefinite wait time (basically, a block). The wait time can also be zero, which allows Poll() to be used for prechecking. The mode is set to one of the SelectMode enumeration values SelectRead, SelectWrite, or SelectError, depending on what we are checking for. Poll() returns true if the socket has an operation pending for the requested mode, or false if it does not.

```
// Block for 1 second waiting for data to read or incoming connections
if (sock.Poll(1000000, SelectMode.SelectRead)) {
    // Socket has data to read or an incoming connection
} else {
    // No data to read or incoming connections
}
```

In general, polling is considered very inefficient because it requires repeated calls to check status. This is sometimes called "busy waiting," because it involves continuously looping back to check for events that probably happen infrequently (at least in relation to the number of checks made). Some ways to avoid polling are discussed later in this chapter, including using the Socket method Select(), which allows blocking on multiple sockets at once (Section 4.2), threads (Section 4.3), and asynchronous I/O (Section 4.4).

A Write() or Send() call blocks until the last byte written is copied into the TCP implementation's local buffer; if the available buffer space is smaller than the size of the write, some data must be successfully transferred to the other end of the connection before the call will return (see Section 5.1 for details). Thus, the amount of time that a large data send may block is controlled by the receiving application. Therefore, any protocol that sends a large enough amount of data over a socket instance can block for an unlimited amount of time. (See Section 5.2 for further discussion on the consequences of this.)

Establishing a Socket connection to a specified host and port will block until either the connection is established, the connection is refused, or a system-imposed timeout occurs. The system-imposed timeout is long (on the order of minutes), and C# does not provide any means of shortening it.

Suppose we want to implement the echo server with a limit on the amount of time taken to service each client. That is, we define a target, TIMELIMIT, and implement the server in such a way that after TIMELIMIT milliseconds, the server instance is terminated.

One approach simply has the server instance keep track of the amount of the remaining time, and use the send and receive timeout settings described above to ensure that reads and writes do not block for longer than that time. TcpEchoServerTimeout.cs implements this approach.

TcpEchoServerTimeout.cs

```
0  using System;              // For Console, Int32, ArgumentException, Environment
1  using System.Net;          // For IPAddress
2  using System.Net.Sockets;  // For TcpListener, TcpClient
3
4  class TcpEchoServerTimeout {
5
6    private const int BUFSIZE = 32;        // Size of receive buffer
```

```
 7   private const int BACKLOG = 5;        // Outstanding conn queue max size
 8   private const int TIMELIMIT = 10000; // Default time limit (ms)
 9
10   static void Main(string[] args) {
11
12     if (args.Length > 1) // Test for correct # of args
13       throw new ArgumentException("Parameters: [<Port>]");
14
15     int servPort = (args.Length == 1) ? Int32.Parse(args[0]): 7;
16
17     Socket server = null;
18
19     try {
20       // Create a socket to accept client connections
21       server = new Socket(AddressFamily.InterNetwork, SocketType.Stream,
22                           ProtocolType.Tcp);
23
24       server.Bind(new IPEndPoint(IPAddress.Any, servPort));
25
26       server.Listen(BACKLOG);
27     } catch (SocketException se) {
28       Console.WriteLine(se.ErrorCode + ": " + se.Message);
29       Environment.Exit(se.ErrorCode);
30     }
31
32     byte[] rcvBuffer = new byte[BUFSIZE]; // Receive buffer
33     int bytesRcvd;                        // Received byte count
34     int totalBytesEchoed = 0;             // Total bytes sent
35
36     for (;;) { // Run forever, accepting and servicing connections
37
38       Socket client = null;
39
40       try {
41
42         client = server.Accept(); // Get client connection
43
44         DateTime starttime = DateTime.Now;
45
46         // Set the ReceiveTimeout
47         client.SetSocketOption(SocketOptionLevel.Socket,
48                                SocketOptionName.ReceiveTimeout,
49                                TIMELIMIT);
```

```
50
51          Console.Write("Handling client at " + client.RemoteEndPoint + " - ");
52
53          // Receive until client closes connection, indicated by 0 return value
54          totalBytesEchoed = 0;
55          while ((bytesRcvd = client.Receive(rcvBuffer, 0, rcvBuffer.Length,
56                                      SocketFlags.None)) > 0) {
57            client.Send(rcvBuffer, 0, bytesRcvd, SocketFlags.None);
58            totalBytesEchoed += bytesRcvd;
59
60            // Check elapsed time
61            TimeSpan elapsed = DateTime.Now - starttime;
62            if (TIMELIMIT - elapsed.TotalMilliseconds < 0) {
63              Console.WriteLine("Aborting client, timelimit " + TIMELIMIT +
64                          "ms exceeded; echoed " + totalBytesEchoed + " bytes");
65              client.Close();
66              throw new SocketException(10060);
67            }
68
69            // Set the ReceiveTimeout
70            client.SetSocketOption(SocketOptionLevel.Socket,
71                                SocketOptionName.ReceiveTimeout,
72                                (int)(TIMELIMIT - elapsed.TotalMilliseconds));
73          }
74          Console.WriteLine("echoed {0} bytes.", totalBytesEchoed);
75
76          client.Close();    // Close the socket. We are done with this client!
77
78        } catch (SocketException se) {
79          if (se.ErrorCode == 10060) { // WSAETIMEDOUT: Connection timed out
80            Console.WriteLine("Aborting client, timelimit " + TIMELIMIT +
81                          "ms exceeded; echoed " + totalBytesEchoed + " bytes");
82          } else {
83            Console.WriteLine(se.ErrorCode + ": " + se.Message);
84          }
85          client.Close();
86        }
87      }
88    }
89 }
```

1. **Argument parsing and setup:** lines 12–17
2. **Create socket, call** Bind() **and** Listen**:** lines 19–30
3. **Main server loop:** lines 36–87
   - **Accept client connection:** line 42
   - **Record start time:** line 44
   - **Set initial timeout:** lines 46–47
     Set the initial Receive() timeout to the TIMELIMIT since minimal time should not have elapsed yet.
   - **Receive loop:** lines 55–73
     Receive data and send echo reply. After each receive and send, update and check the elapsed time and abort if necessary. To abort we throw the same exception a timeout during the Receive() would throw, which is a SocketException with ErrorCode 10060. If we have not exceeded our timeout after the data transfer, reset the Receive() timeout based on our new elapsed time before we loop around to receive more data.
   - **Successful completion:** lines 74–76
     If we successfully echo all the bytes within the timelimit, output the echoed byte length and close the client socket.
   - **Exception handling:** lines 78–86
     If we hit a timeout limit, output the appropriate message. Close the client socket and allow the receive loop to continue and handle more clients.

4.1.3   Nonblocking Sockets

One solution to the problem of undesirable blocking is to change the behavior of the socket so that all calls are *nonblocking*. For such a socket, if a requested operation can be completed immediately the call's return will succeed. If the requested operation cannot be completed immediately, it throws a SocketException with the ErrorCode property set to 10035 with a Message of "Operation would block." The standard approach is to catch this exception, continue with processing, and try again later.

The Socket class contains a Blocking property that, when set to false, causes all methods on that socket that would normally block until their operation completed to no longer block. Like polling, nonblocking sockets typically involve some busy-waiting and are not very efficient. Better methods to implement this are discussed with Select() (Section 4.2), threads (Section 4.3), and asynchronous I/O (Section 4.4)

Here we present a version of the TcpEchoClient.cs program from Chapter 2 that has been modified to use a nonblocking socket. An alternative version that utilizes the Poll() method instead is also available on the book's website (www.mkp.com/practical/csharpsockets).

TcpNBEchoClient.cs

```
0   using System;              // For String, Environment
1   using System.Text;         // For Encoding
2   using System.IO;           // For IOException
3   using System.Net;          // For IPEndPoint, Dns
4   using System.Net.Sockets;  // For TcpClient, NetworkStream, SocketException
5   using System.Threading;    // For Thread.Sleep
6
7   public class TcpNBEchoClient {
8
9     static void Main(string[] args) {
10
11      if ((args.Length < 2) || (args.Length > 3)) // Test for correct # of args
12        throw new ArgumentException("Parameters: <Server> <Word> [<Port>]");
13
14      String server = args[0]; // Server name or IP address
15
16      // Convert input String to bytes
17      byte[] byteBuffer = Encoding.ASCII.GetBytes(args[1]);
18
19      // Use port argument if supplied, otherwise default to 7
20      int servPort = (args.Length == 3) ? Int32.Parse(args[2]) : 7;
21
22      // Create Socket and connect
23      Socket sock = null;
24      try {
25        sock = new Socket(AddressFamily.InterNetwork, SocketType.Stream,
26                          ProtocolType.Tcp);
27
28        sock.Connect(new IPEndPoint(Dns.Resolve(server).AddressList[0], servPort));
29      } catch (Exception e) {
30        Console.WriteLine(e.Message);
31        Environment.Exit(-1);
32      }
33
34      // Receive the same string back from the server
35      int totalBytesSent = 0; // Total bytes sent so far
36      int totalBytesRcvd = 0; // Total bytes received so far
37
38      // Make sock a nonblocking Socket
39      sock.Blocking = false;
40
```

```
41      // Loop until all bytes have been echoed by server
42      while (totalBytesRcvd < byteBuffer.Length) {
43
44        // Send the encoded string to the server
45        if (totalBytesSent < byteBuffer.Length) {
46          try {
47            totalBytesSent += sock.Send(byteBuffer, totalBytesSent,
48                                        byteBuffer.Length - totalBytesSent,
49                                        SocketFlags.None);
50            Console.WriteLine("Sent a total of {0} bytes to server...", totalBytesSent);
51
52          } catch (SocketException se) {
53            if (se.ErrorCode == 10035) {//WSAEWOULDBLOCK: Resource temporarily unavailable
54              Console.WriteLine("Temporarily unable to send, will retry again later.");
55            } else {
56              Console.WriteLine(se.ErrorCode + ": " + se.Message);
57              sock.Close();
58              Environment.Exit(se.ErrorCode);
59            }
60          }
61        }
62
63        try {
64          int bytesRcvd = 0;
65          if ((bytesRcvd = sock.Receive(byteBuffer, totalBytesRcvd,
66                                        byteBuffer.Length - totalBytesRcvd,
67                                        SocketFlags.None)) == 0) {
68            Console.WriteLine("Connection closed prematurely.");
69            break;
70          }
71          totalBytesRcvd += bytesRcvd;
72        } catch (SocketException se) {
73          if (se.ErrorCode == 10035)//WSAEWOULDBLOCK: Resource temporarily unavailable
74            continue;
75          else {
76            Console.WriteLine(se.ErrorCode + ": " + se.Message);
77            break;
78          }
79        }
80        doThing();
81      }
82      Console.WriteLine("Received {0} bytes from server: {1}", totalBytesRcvd,
83                        Encoding.ASCII.GetString(byteBuffer, 0, totalBytesRcvd));
```

```
84
85        sock.Close();
86    }
87
88    static void doThing() {
89        Console.Write(".");
90        Thread.Sleep(2000);
91    }
92  }
```

TcpNBEchoClient.cs

1. **Setup and argument parsing:** lines 11–20
2. Socket **and** IPEndPoint **setup:** lines 22–32
   Create a Socket instance, create an IPEndPoint instance for the server from the command-line parameters, and connect to the server.
3. **Set** Blocking **to** false**:** lines 38–39
4. **Main loop:** lines 41–81
   - **Loop until all bytes sent have been echoed:** line 42
   - **Send bytes to server:** lines 44–50
     In case all bytes cannot be sent in one send, continue trying to send until the number of bytes sent matches the send byte buffer size.
   - **Handle exceptions:** lines 52–60
     If we get a SocketException with an ErrorCode of 10035, the send would have blocked. This is not necessarily a fatal error, so we output an informational message and allow the loop to continue.
   - **Receive echo reply:** lines 63–79
     Attempt to do a Receive() in nonblocking mode. If there is no data to receive, a SocketException is thrown with ErrorCode set to 10035. As per normal Receive() semantics, a Receive() return of 0 indicates that the remote server has closed the connection. Other processing is simulated here by method doThing().
5. **Output echo reply and close socket:** lines 82–86

4.2 **Multiplexing**

4.2.1 The Socket Select() Method

Our programs so far have dealt with I/O over a single channel; each version of our echo server deals with only one client connection at a time. However, it is often the case that an application needs the ability to do I/O on multiple channels simultaneously. For example, we might want to provide echo service on several ports at once. The problem with this becomes clear as soon as you consider what happens after the server creates and binds a socket to each port. It is ready to Accept() connections, but which socket to choose? A call to Accept() or Receive() on one socket may block, causing established connections to another socket to wait unnecessarily. This problem can be solved using nonblocking sockets, but in that case the server ends up continually polling the sockets, which is wasteful. We would like to let the server block until *some* socket is ready for I/O.

Fortunately the socket API provides a way to do this. With the static Socket Select() method, a program can specify a list of sockets to check for pending I/O; Select() suspends the program until one or more of the sockets in the list becomes ready to perform I/O. The list is modified to only include those Socket instances that are ready.

Select() takes four arguments, the first three of which are lists of Sockets, and the fourth of which is a time in *microseconds* (not milliseconds) indicating how long to wait. A negative value on the wait time indicates an indefinite wait period. The socket lists can be any class that implements the IList interface (this includes ArrayList, used in our example). The lists represent what event you are waiting for; in order, they represent checking read readiness, write readiness, and error existence. The lists should be populated with references to the Socket instances prior to call. When the call completes, the lists will contain only the Socket references that meet that list's criteria (readability, writability, or error existence). If you don't want to check for all these conditions in a single Select() call, you can pass null for up to two of the lists.

Let's reconsider the problem of running the echo service on multiple ports. If we create a socket for each port, we could list those Sockets in an ArrayList. A call to Select(), given such a list, would suspend the program until an echo request arrives for at least one of our sockets. We could then handle the connection setup and echo for that particular socket. Our next example, TcpEchoServerSelect.cs, implements this model. The server runs on three ports: 8080, 8081, and 8082.

TcpEchoServerSelectSocket.cs

```
0   using System;              // For Console, Int32, ArgumentException, Environment
1   using System.Net;          // For IPAddress
2   using System.Collections;  // For ArrayList
3   using System.Net.Sockets;  // For Socket, SocketException
4
5   class TcpEchoServerSelectSocket {
6
7     private const int BUFSIZE = 32;         // Size of receive buffer
8     private const int BACKLOG = 5;          // Outstanding conn queue max size
9     private const int SERVER1_PORT = 8080;  // Port for second echo server
10    private const int SERVER2_PORT = 8081;  // Port for second echo server
```

```
11      private const int SERVER3_PORT = 8082;      // Port for third echo server
12      private const int SELECT_WAIT_TIME = 1000; // Microsecs for Select() to wait
13
14      static void Main(string[] args) {
15
16        Socket server1 = null;
17        Socket server2 = null;
18        Socket server3 = null;
19
20        try {
21          // Create a socket to accept client connections
22          server1 = new Socket(AddressFamily.InterNetwork, SocketType.Stream,
23                               ProtocolType.Tcp);
24          server2 = new Socket(AddressFamily.InterNetwork, SocketType.Stream,
25                               ProtocolType.Tcp);
26          server3 = new Socket(AddressFamily.InterNetwork, SocketType.Stream,
27                               ProtocolType.Tcp);
28
29          server1.Bind(new IPEndPoint(IPAddress.Any, SERVER1_PORT));
30          server2.Bind(new IPEndPoint(IPAddress.Any, SERVER2_PORT));
31          server3.Bind(new IPEndPoint(IPAddress.Any, SERVER3_PORT));
32
33          server1.Listen(BACKLOG);
34          server2.Listen(BACKLOG);
35          server3.Listen(BACKLOG);
36        } catch (SocketException se) {
37          Console.WriteLine(se.ErrorCode + ": " + se.Message);
38          Environment.Exit(se.ErrorCode);
39        }
40
41        byte[] rcvBuffer = new byte[BUFSIZE]; // Receive buffer
42        int bytesRcvd;                        // Received byte count
43
44        for (;;) { // Run forever, accepting and servicing connections
45
46          Socket client = null;
47
48          // Create an array list of all three sockets
49          ArrayList acceptList = new ArrayList();
50          acceptList.Add(server1);
51          acceptList.Add(server2);
52          acceptList.Add(server3);
53
```

```
54        try {
55
56          // The Select call will check readable status of each socket
57          // in the list
58          Socket.Select(acceptList, null, null, SELECT_WAIT_TIME);
59
60          // The acceptList will now contain ONLY the server sockets with
61          // pending connections:
62          for (int i=0; i < acceptList.Count; i++) {
63            client = ((Socket)acceptList[i]).Accept(); // Get client connection
64
65            IPEndPoint localEP = (IPEndPoint)((Socket)acceptList[i]).LocalEndPoint;
66            Console.Write("Server port " + localEP.Port);
67            Console.Write(" - handling client at " + client.RemoteEndPoint + " - ");
68
69            // Receive until client closes connection, indicated by 0 return value
70            int totalBytesEchoed = 0;
71            while ((bytesRcvd = client.Receive(rcvBuffer, 0, rcvBuffer.Length,
72                                               SocketFlags.None)) > 0) {
73              client.Send(rcvBuffer, 0, bytesRcvd, SocketFlags.None);
74              totalBytesEchoed += bytesRcvd;
75            }
76            Console.WriteLine("echoed {0} bytes.", totalBytesEchoed);
77
78            client.Close();   // Close the socket. We are done with this client!
79          }
80
81        } catch (Exception e) {
82          Console.WriteLine(e.Message);
83          client.Close();
84        }
85      }
86    }
87  }
```

TcpEchoServerSelectSocket.cs

1. **Constant definition:** lines 7–12
   Define the three ports the echo server will respond to.

2. **Create, bind, and listen on all three socket ports:** lines 20–39
   All of these calls are nonblocking by default.

3. **Main server loop:** lines 44–85
   - ■ **Put the socket instances into an** ArrayList**:** lines 48–52
   - ■ Select(): lines 56–58
     Use the ArrayList of sockets as input to the Select() call. As the first input the sockets in the array will be checked for incoming connections, and any sockets without connections will be removed from the list.
   - ■ **Loop through and process incoming connections:** lines 60–79
     From this point on the processing is the same as in our previous examples. Each socket in the array has its Accept() method called to retrieve the client Socket. The client socket's Receive() and Send() methods are called to read and echo the data, and the socket is closed when complete.

4.3   Threads

In the preceding section we demonstrated how to use the nonblocking I/O features of .NET to run other code while waiting on socket operations. There are two main drawbacks to this nonblocking approach. First, polling for completion of socket methods is fairly inefficient. If you don't poll soon enough, time is lost after the socket operation completes. If you poll too soon, the operation will not be ready and you'll either have to block or check back again later.

Second, the number of connections that can be handled concurrently is limited. If a client connects while another is already being serviced, the server will not echo the new client's data until it has finished with the current client, although the new client will be able to send data as soon as it connects. This type of server is known as an *iterative server*. Iterative servers handle clients sequentially, finishing with one client before servicing the next. They work best for applications where each client requires a small, bounded amount of server connection time; however, if the time to handle a client can be long, the wait experienced by subsequent clients may be unacceptable.

To demonstrate the problem, add a 10-second sleep using Thread.Sleep(10000)[1] after the TcpClient connect call in TcpEchoClient.cs and experiment with several clients simultaneously accessing the TCP echo server. Here the sleep operation simulates an operation that takes significant time, such as slow file or network I/O. Note that a new client must wait for all already-connected clients to complete before it gets service.

What we need is some way for each connection to proceed independently, without interfering with other connections. That is where implementing *threads* comes in. Thread programming is a very complex topic in itself and beyond the scope of this book, but for our purposes you can conceptually think of threads as portions of code that can execute concurrently. This allows one "thread of execution" to block on an operation while another thread continues to run.

---

[1] You will need to add "using System.Threading;" at the beginning of the program.

The .NET API provides System.Threading class library for implementing threads. The .NET threading capabilities are very flexible and allow a program to handle many network connections simultaneously. Using threads, a single application can work on several tasks concurrently. In our echo server, we can give responsibility for each client to an independently executing thread. All of the examples we have seen so far consist of a single thread, which simply executes the Main() method. In this section we describe two approaches to coding *concurrent servers*, namely, *thread-per-client*, where a new thread is spawned to handle each client connection, and *thread pool*, where a fixed, prespawned set of threads work together to handle client connections.

To create a new thread in C# you create a new instance of the Thread class, which as its argument takes a *delegate* method that will operate in its own thread. This thread delegate is represented by the ThreadStart class, which takes the method to be run as its argument. Once the Thread has been instantiated, the Start() method is called to begin execution on that thread. For example, if you have created a method called runMyThread(), the code to create and start the code running as its own thread would be:

```
using System.Threading;
⋮

// Create a ThreadStart instance using your method as a delegate:
ThreadStart methodDelegate = new ThreadStart(runMyThread);

// Create a Thread instance using your delegate method:
Thread t = new Thread(methodDelegate);

// Start the thread
t.Start();
```

The new thread does not begin execution until its Start() method is invoked. When the Start() method of an instance of Thread is invoked, the CLR causes the specified method to be executed in a new thread, concurrently with all others. Meanwhile, the *original* thread returns from its call to Start() and continues its execution independently. (Note that directly calling the method without passing it to a Thread via a delegate has the normal procedure-call semantics: the method is executed in the caller's thread.) The exact interleaving of thread execution is determined by several factors, including the implementation of the CLR, the load, the underlying OS, and the host configuration. For example, on a uniprocessor system, threads share the processor sequentially; on a multiprocessor system, multiple threads from the same application can run simultaneously on different processors.

Note that the method delegate cannot take any arguments or return a value. Luckily, there are mechanisms to circumvent both of these limitations. To pass arguments into a Thread instance while maintaining data encapsulation, you could break your separate thread code into its own class. For example, suppose you want to pass an instance of TcpClient into your runMyThread() method. You could create a new class (e.g., MyThread-Class) that contained the runMyThread() method, and pass the TcpClient instance into the class constructor. Then when you use a Thread to start the runMyThread() method, it can access the TcpClient instance via a local variable.

To get data back from a Thread instance you need to set up a callback delegate method. The Thread instance will then invoke this callback method to pass the data back. The details of setting up a callback method are beyond the scope of this book; check the MSDN library under System.Threading for more details.

We illustrate the approach of passing data to a Thread in a simple example that runs a method of class instance MyThreadClass in its own thread. The method repeatedly prints a greeting to the system output stream. The string greeting is passed as a parameter to the class constructor, where it is stored as a class instance variable and accessed by the thread when it is invoked.

ThreadExample.cs

```
0   using System;           // For String
1   using System.Threading;  // For Thread
2
3   class MyThreadClass {
4     // Class that takes a String greeting as input, then outputs that
5     // greeting to the console 10 times in its own thread with a random
6     // interval between each greeting.
7
8     private const int RANDOM_SLEEP_MAX = 500; // Max random milliseconds to sleep
9     private const int LOOP_COUNT = 10;         // Number of times to print message
10
11    private String greeting;   // Message to print to console
12
13    public MyThreadClass(String greeting) {
14      this.greeting = greeting;
15    }
16
17    public void runMyThread() {
18      Random rand = new Random();
19
20      for (int x=0; x < LOOP_COUNT; x++) {
21        Console.WriteLine("Thread-" + Thread.CurrentThread.GetHashCode() + ": " +
22                          greeting);
23        try {
24          // Sleep 0 to RANDOM_SLEEP_MAX milliseconds
25          Thread.Sleep(rand.Next(RANDOM_SLEEP_MAX));
26        } catch (ThreadInterruptedException) {}  // Will not happen
27      }
```

```
28    }
29  }
30
31  class ThreadExample {
32
33    static void Main(string[] args) {
34
35      MyThreadClass mtc1 = new MyThreadClass("Hello");
36      new Thread(new ThreadStart(mtc1.runMyThread)).Start();
37
38      MyThreadClass mtc2 = new MyThreadClass("Aloha");
39      new Thread(new ThreadStart(mtc2.runMyThread)).Start();
40
41      MyThreadClass mtc3 = new MyThreadClass("Ciao");
42      new Thread(new ThreadStart(mtc3.runMyThread)).Start();
43    }
44  }
```

ThreadExample.cs

1. MyThreadClass: lines 3–29
   In order to pass state to the method we will be running as its own thread, we put the method in its own class, and pass the state variables in the class constructor. In this case the state is the string greeting to be printed.
   - **Constructor:** lines 13–15
     Each instance of ThreadExample contains its own greeting string.
   - **Initialize an instance of** Random(): line 18
     Used to generate a random number of sleep times.
   - for **loop:** line 20
     Loop 10 times.
   - **Print the thread id and instance greeting:** lines 21–22
     The static method Thread.CurrentThread.GetHashCode() returns a unique id reference to the thread from which it is called.
   - **Suspend thread:** lines 24–26
     After printing its instance's greeting message, each thread sleeps for a random amount of time (between 0 and 500 milliseconds) by calling the static method Thread.Sleep(), which takes the number of milliseconds to sleep as a parameter. The rand.Next(500) call returns a random **int** between 0 and 500. Thread.Sleep() can be interrupted by another thread, in which case ThreadInterruptedException is thrown. Our example does not include an interrupt call, so the exception will not happen in this application.

2. Main(): lines 33–43

Each of the three groupings of statements in Main() does the following: (1) creates a new instance of MyThreadClass with a different greeting string; (2) passes the runMyThread() method of the new instance to the constructor of ThreadStart; (3) passes the ThreadStart instance to the constructor of Thread; and (4) calls the new Thread instance's Start() method. Each thread independently executes the runMyThread() method of ThreadExample, while the Main() thread terminates.

Upon execution, an interleaving of the three greeting messages is printed to the console. The exact interleaving of the numbers depends upon the factors mentioned earlier.

4.3.1   Server Protocol

Since the two server approaches we are going to describe (thread-per-client and thread pool) are independent of the particular client-server protocol, we want to be able to use the same protocol code for both. In order to make the protocol used easily extensible, the protocol classes will implement the IProtocol interface, defined in IProtocol.cs. This simple interface has only one method, handleclient(), which has no arguments and a void return type.

IProtocol.cs

```
0   public interface IProtocol {
1     void handleclient();
2   }
```

The code for the echo protocol is given in the class EchoProtocol, which encapsulates the implementation of the server side of the echo protocol. The idea is that the server creates a separate instance of EchoProtocol for each connection, and protocol execution begins when handleclient() is called on an instance. The code in handleclient() is almost identical to the connection handling code in TcpEchoServer.cs, except that a logging capability (described shortly) has been added. We can create a thread that independently executes handleclient(), or we can invoke handleclient() directly.

EchoProtocol.cs

```
0   using System.Collections;    // For ArrayList
1   using System.Threading;      // For Thread
2   using System.Net.Sockets;    // For Socket
```

```
3
4    class EchoProtocol : IProtocol {
5      public const int BUFSIZE = 32; // Byte size of IO buffer
6
7      private Socket clntSock;  // Connection socket
8      private ILogger logger;    // Logging facility
9
10     public EchoProtocol(Socket clntSock, ILogger logger) {
11       this.clntSock = clntSock;
12       this.logger = logger;
13     }
14
15     public void handleclient() {
16       ArrayList entry = new ArrayList();
17       entry.Add("Client address and port = " + clntSock.RemoteEndPoint);
18       entry.Add("Thread = " + Thread.CurrentThread.GetHashCode());
19
20       try {
21         // Receive until client closes connection, indicated by a SocketException
22         int recvMsgSize;                        // Size of received message
23         int totalBytesEchoed = 0;               // Bytes received from client
24         byte[] rcvBuffer = new byte[BUFSIZE]; // Receive buffer
25
26         // Receive untl client closes connection, indicated by 0 return code
27         try {
28           while ((recvMsgSize = clntSock.Receive(rcvBuffer, 0, rcvBuffer.Length,
29                   SocketFlags.None)) > 0) {
30             clntSock.Send(rcvBuffer, 0, recvMsgSize, SocketFlags.None);
31             totalBytesEchoed += recvMsgSize;
32           }
33         } catch (SocketException se) {
34           entry.Add(se.ErrorCode + ": " + se.Message);
35         }
36
37         entry.Add("Client finished; echoed " + totalBytesEchoed + " bytes.");
38       } catch (SocketException se) {
39         entry.Add(se.ErrorCode + ": " +  se.Message);
40       }
41
42       clntSock.Close();
43
44       logger.writeEntry(entry);
```

```
45    }
46  }
```

1. **Member variables and constructor:** lines 5–13
   Each instance of EchoProtocol contains a client socket for the connection and a reference to the logger.

2. handleclient(): lines 15–45
   Handle a single client:
   - **Write the client and thread information to the log:** lines 16–18
     ArrayList is a dynamically sized container of Objects. The Add() method of ArrayList inserts the specified object at the end of the list. In this case, the inserted object is a String. Each element of the ArrayList represents a line of output to the logger.
   - **Execute the echo protocol:** lines 20–42
   - **Write the elements (one per line) of the** ArrayList **instance to the logger:** line 44

The logger allows for synchronized reporting of thread creation and client completion, so that entries from different threads are not interleaved. This facility is defined by the ILogger interface, which has methods for writing strings or object collections.

ILogger.cs

```
0  using System;              // For String
1  using System.Collections;  // For ArrayList
2
3  public interface ILogger {
4    void writeEntry(ArrayList entry); // Write list of lines
5    void writeEntry(String entry);    // Write single line
6  }
```

writeEntry() logs the given string or object collection. How it is logged depends on the implementation. One possibility is to send the log messages to the console.

ConsoleLogger.cs

```
0  using System;              // For String
1  using System.Collections;  // For ArrayList
```

```
2  using System.Threading;     // For Mutex
3
4  class ConsoleLogger : ILogger {
5    private static Mutex mutex = new Mutex();
6
7    public void writeEntry(ArrayList entry) {
8      mutex.WaitOne();
9
10     IEnumerator line = entry.GetEnumerator();
11     while (line.MoveNext())
12        Console.WriteLine(line.Current);
13
14     Console.WriteLine();
15
16     mutex.ReleaseMutex();
17   }
18
19   public void writeEntry(String entry) {
20     mutex.WaitOne();
21
22     Console.WriteLine(entry);
23     Console.WriteLine();
24
25     mutex.ReleaseMutex();
26   }
27 }
```

ConsoleLogger.cs

Another possibility is to write the log messages to a file specified in the constructor, as in the following example.

FileLogger.cs

```
0  using System;               // For String
1  using System.IO;            // For StreamWriter
2  using System.Threading;     // For Mutex
3  using System.Collections;   // For ArrayList
4
5  class FileLogger : ILogger {
6    private static Mutex mutex = new Mutex();
7
```

```
 8    private StreamWriter output;   // Log file
 9
10    public FileLogger(String filename) {
11      // Create log file
12      output = new StreamWriter(filename, true);
13    }
14
15    public void writeEntry(ArrayList entry) {
16      mutex.WaitOne();
17
18      IEnumerator line = entry.GetEnumerator();
19      while (line.MoveNext())
20        output.WriteLine(line.Current);
21      output.WriteLine();
22      output.Flush();
23
24      mutex.ReleaseMutex();
25    }
26
27    public void writeEntry(String entry) {
28      mutex.WaitOne();
29
30      output.WriteLine(entry);
31      output.WriteLine();
32      output.Flush();
33
34      mutex.ReleaseMutex();
35    }
36  }
```

FileLogger.cs

In each example the System.Threading.Mutex class is used to guarantee that only one thread is writing at one time.

We are now ready to introduce some different approaches to concurrent servers.

4.3.2 Thread-per-Client

In a *thread-per-client* server, a new thread is created to handle each connection. The server executes a loop that runs forever, listening for connections on a specified port and repeatedly accepting an incoming connection from a client, and then spawning a new thread to handle that connection.

TcpEchoServerThread.cs implements the thread-per-client architecture. It is very similar to the iterative server, using a single indefinite loop to receive and process client requests. The main difference is that it creates a thread to handle the connection instead of handling it directly.

TcpEchoServerThread.cs

```
0   using System;                // For Int32, ArgumentException
1   using System.Threading;      // For Thread
2   using System.Net;            // For IPAddress
3   using System.Net.Sockets;    // For TcpListener, Socket
4
5   class TcpEchoServerThread {
6
7     static void Main(string[] args) {
8
9       if (args.Length != 1)  // Test for correct # of args
10        throw new ArgumentException("Parameter(s): <Port>");
11
12      int echoServPort = Int32.Parse(args[0]);  // Server port
13
14      // Create a TcpListener socket to accept client connection requests
15      TcpListener listener = new TcpListener(IPAddress.Any, echoServPort);
16
17      ILogger logger = new ConsoleLogger();  // Log messages to console
18
19      listener.Start();
20
21      // Run forever, accepting and spawning threads to service each connection
22      for (;;) {
23        try {
24          Socket clntSock = listener.AcceptSocket(); // Block waiting for connection
25          EchoProtocol protocol = new EchoProtocol(clntSock, logger);
26          Thread thread = new Thread(new ThreadStart(protocol.handleclient));
27          thread.Start();
28          logger.writeEntry("Created and started Thread = " + thread.GetHashCode());
29        } catch (System.IO.IOException e) {
30          logger.writeEntry("Exception = " + e.Message);
31        }
32      }
```

```
33      /* NOT REACHED */
34   }
35 }
```

---

1. **Parameter parsing and server socket/logger creation:** lines 9–19

2. **Loop forever, handling incoming connections:** lines 21–33

   ■ **Accept an incoming connection:** line 24

   ■ **Create a protocol instance to handle new connection:** line 25
   Each connection gets its own instance of EchoProtocol. Each instance maintains the state of its particular connection. The echo protocol has little internal state, but more sophisticated protocols may require substantial amounts of state.

   ■ **Create, start, and log a new thread for the connection:** lines 26–28
   Since EchoProtocol implements a method suitable for execution as a thread (handleclient() in this case, a method that takes no parameters and returns void), we can give our new instance's thread method to the ThreadStart constructor, which in turn is passed to the Thread constructor. The new thread will execute the handleclient() method of EchoProtocol when Start() is invoked. The GetHashCode() method of the static Thread.CurrentThread property returns a unique id number for the new thread.

   ■ **Handle exception from** AcceptSocket(): lines 29–31
   If some I/O error occurs, AcceptSocket() throws a SocketException. In our earlier iterative echo server (TcpEchoServer.cs), the exception is not handled, and such an error terminates the server. Here we handle the exception by logging the error and continuing execution.

4.3.3 Factoring the Server

Our threaded server does what we want it to, but the code is not very reusable or extensible. First, the echo protocol is hard-coded in the server. What if we want an HTTP server instead? We could write an HTTPProtocol and replace the instantiation of EchoProtocol in Main(); however, we would have to revise Main() and have a separate main class for each different protocol that we implement.

We want to be able to instantiate a protocol instance of the appropriate type for each connection without knowing any specifics about the protocol, including the name of a constructor. This problem—instantiating an object without knowing details about its type—arises frequently in object-oriented programming, and there is a standard solution: use a *factory*. A factory object supplies instances of a particular class, hiding the details of how the instance is created, such as what constructor is used.

For our protocol factory, we define the IProtocolFactory interface to have a single method, createProtocol(), which takes Socket and ILogger instances as arguments and returns an instance implementing the desired protocol. Our protocols will all implement the handleclient() method, so we can run them as their own Thread to execute the protocol for that connection. Thus, our protocol factory returns instances that implement the handleclient() method:

IProtocolFactory.cs

```
0  using System.Net.Sockets;   // For Socket
1
2  public interface IProtocolFactory {
3    IProtocol createProtocol(Socket clntSock, ILogger logger);
4  }
```

IProtocolFactory.cs

We now need to implement a protocol factory for the echo protocol. The factory class is simple. All it does is return a new instance of EchoProtocol whenever createProtocol() is called.

EchoProtocolFactory.cs

```
0  using System.Net.Sockets; // For Socket
1
2  public class EchoProtocolFactory : IProtocolFactory {
3    public EchoProtocolFactory() {}
4
5    public IProtocol createProtocol(Socket clntSock, ILogger logger) {
6      return new EchoProtocol(clntSock, logger);
7    }
8  }
```

EchoProtocolFactory.cs

We have factored out some of the details of protocol instance creation from our server, so that the various iterative and concurrent servers can reuse the protocol code. However, the server approach (iterative, thread-per-client, etc.) is still hard-coded in Main(). These server approaches deal with how to *dispatch* each connection to the appropriate handling mechanism. To provide greater extensibility, we want to factor out the dispatching model from the Main() of TcpEchoServerThread.cs so that we can use any dispatching model with any protocol. Since we have many potential dispatching models, we define the IDispatcher interface to hide the particulars of the threading strategy from the rest of the server code. It contains a single method, startDispatching(), which tells the dispatcher to start handling clients accepted via the given TcpListener, creating protocol instances using the given IProtocolFactory, and logging via the given ILogger.

IDispatcher.cs

```
0  using System.Net.Sockets;  // For TcpListener
1
2  public interface IDispatcher {
3    void startDispatching(TcpListener listener, ILogger logger,
4                          IProtocolFactory protoFactory);
5  }
```

IDispatcher.cs

To implement the thread-per-client dispatcher, we simply pull the for loop from Main() in TcpEchoServerThread.cs into the startDispatching() method of the new dispatcher. The only other change we need to make is to use the protocol factory instead of instantiating a particular protocol.

ThreadPerDispatcher.cs

```
0  using System.Net.Sockets; // For TcpListener, Socket
1  using System.Threading;   // For Thread
2
3  class ThreadPerDispatcher : IDispatcher {
4
5    public void startDispatching(TcpListener listener, ILogger logger,
6                          IProtocolFactory protoFactory) {
7
8      // Run forever, accepting and spawning threads to service each connection
9
10     for (;;) {
11       try {
12         listener.Start();
13         Socket clntSock = listener.AcceptSocket();  // Block waiting for connection
14         IProtocol protocol = protoFactory.createProtocol(clntSock, logger);
15         Thread thread = new Thread(new ThreadStart(protocol.handleclient));
16         thread.Start();
17         logger.writeEntry("Created and started Thread = " + thread.GetHashCode());
```

```
18          } catch (System.IO.IOException e) {
19              logger.writeEntry("Exception = " + e.Message);
20          }
21      }
22      /* NOT REACHED */
23    }
24  }
```

ThreadPerDispatcher.cs

We demonstrate the use of this dispatcher and protocol factory in ThreadMain.cs, which we introduce after discussing the thread-pool approach to dispatching.

4.3.4 Thread Pool

Every new thread consumes system resources; spawning a thread takes CPU cycles and each thread has its own data structures (e.g., stacks) that consume system memory. In addition, the scheduling and context switching among threads creates extra work. As the number of threads increases, more and more system resources are consumed by thread overhead. Eventually, the system is spending more time dealing with thread management than with servicing connections. At that point, adding an additional thread may actually *increase* client service time.

We can avoid this problem by limiting the total number of threads and reusing threads. Instead of spawning a new thread for each connection, the server creates a *thread pool* on startup by spawning a fixed number of threads. When a new client connection arrives at the server, it is assigned to a thread from the pool. When the thread finishes with the client, it returns to the pool, ready to handle another request. Connection requests that arrive when all threads in the pool are busy are queued to be serviced by the next available thread.

Like the thread-per-client server, a thread-pool server begins by creating a Tcp-Listener. Then it spawns *N* threads, each of which loops forever, accepting connections from the (shared) TcpListener instance. When multiple threads simultaneously call AcceptSocket() on the same TcpListener instance, they all block until a connection is established. Then the system selects one thread, and the Socket instance for the new connection is returned *only in that thread*. The other threads remain blocked until the next connection is established and another lucky winner is chosen.

Since each thread in the pool loops forever, processing connections one by one, a thread-pool server is really a set of iterative servers. Unlike the thread-per-client server, a thread-pool thread does not terminate when it finishes with a client. Instead, it starts over again, blocking on AcceptSocket().

A thread pool is simply a different model for dispatching connection requests, so all we really need to do is write another dispatcher. PoolDispatcher.cs implements our thread-pool dispatcher. To see how the thread-pool server would be implemented without dispatchers and protocol factories, see `TCPEchoServerPool.cs` on the book's website (www.mkp.com/practical/csharpsockets).

PoolDispatcher.cs

```
0   using System.Threading;    // For Thread
1   using System.Net.Sockets;  // For TcpListener
2
3   class PoolDispatcher : IDispatcher {
4
5     private const int NUMTHREADS = 8;   // Default thread pool size
6
7     private int numThreads;             // Number of threads in pool
8
9     public PoolDispatcher() {
10      this.numThreads = NUMTHREADS;
11    }
12
13    public PoolDispatcher(int numThreads) {
14      this.numThreads = numThreads;
15    }
16
17    public void startDispatching(TcpListener listener, ILogger logger,
18                          IProtocolFactory protoFactory) {
19      // Create N threads, each running an iterative server
20      for (int i = 0; i < numThreads; i++) {
21        DispatchLoop dl = new DispatchLoop(listener, logger, protoFactory);
22        Thread thread = new Thread(new ThreadStart(dl.rundispatcher));
23        thread.Start();
24        logger.writeEntry("Created and started Thread = " + thread.GetHashCode());
25      }
26    }
27  }
28
29  class DispatchLoop {
30
31    TcpListener listener;
32    ILogger logger;
33    IProtocolFactory protoFactory;
34
35    public DispatchLoop(TcpListener listener, ILogger logger,
36                    IProtocolFactory protoFactory) {
37      this.listener    = listener;
```

```
38      this.logger     = logger;
39      this.protoFactory = protoFactory;
40    }
41
42    public void rundispatcher() {
43      // Run forever, accepting and handling each connection
44      for (;;) {
45        try {
46          Socket clntSock = listener.AcceptSocket(); // Block waiting for connection
47          IProtocol protocol = protoFactory.createProtocol(clntSock, logger);
48          protocol.handleclient();
49        } catch (SocketException se) {
50          logger.writeEntry("Exception = " +  se.Message);
51        }
52      }
53    }
54  }
```

PoolDispatcher.cs

1. `PoolDispatcher()`: lines 9–15
   The thread-pool solution needs an additional piece of information: the number of threads in the pool. We need to provide this information to the instance before the thread pool is constructed. We could pass the number of threads to the constructor, but this limits our options because the constructor interface varies by dispatcher. We allow the option to pass the number of threads in the constructor, but if none is passed, a default of 8 is used.

2. `startDispatching()`: lines 17–26
   ▪ **Spawn *N* threads to execute instances of** `DispatchLoop`: lines 17–26
     For each loop iteration, an instance of the `DispatchLoop` class is instantiated with a constructor that takes a `TcpListener`, a `ILogger`, and a `IProtocolFactory`. The `rundispatcher()` method of the `DispatchLoop` is then run as its own thread. When the `Start()` method is called, the thread executes the `rundispatcher()` method of the `DispatchLoop` class. The `rundispatcher()` method in turn runs the protocol, which implements an iterative server.

3. `DispatchLoop` **class:** lines 29–54
   The constructor stores copies of the `TcpListener`, `ILogger`, and `IProtocolFactory`. The `rundispatcher()` method loops forever, executing:
   ▪ **Accept an incoming connection:** line 46
     Since there are *N* threads executing `rundispatcher()`, up to *N* threads can be blocked on *listener*'s `AcceptSocket()`, waiting for an incoming connection.

The system ensures that only one thread gets a Socket for any particular connection. If no threads are blocked on AcceptSocket() when a client connection is established, the new connection is queued until the next call to AcceptSocket() (see Section 5.4.1).

- **Create a protocol instance to handle new connection:** line 47
- **Run the protocol for the connection:** line 48
- **Handle exception from** AcceptSocket(): lines 49–51

Since threads are reused, the thread-pool solution only pays the overhead of thread creation *N* times, irrespective of the total number of client connections. Since we control the maximum number of simultaneously executing threads, we can control scheduling overhead. Spawning too many threads is not good either, as each additional thread consumes resources and can overload an operating system. Of course, if we spawn too few threads, we can still have clients waiting a long time for service; therefore, the size of the thread pool should be tuned so that client connection time is minimized.

The Main() of ThreadMain.cs demonstrates how to use either the thread-per-client or thread-pool server. This application takes three parameters: (1) the port number for the server, (2) the protocol name (use "Echo" for the echo protocol), and (3) the dispatcher name (use "ThreadPer" or "Pool" for the thread-per-client and thread-pool servers, respectively). The number of threads for the thread pool defaults to 8.

```
C:\> ThreadMain 5000 Echo Pool
```

ThreadMain.cs

```
0  using System;              // For String, Int32, Activator
1  using System.Net;          // For IPAddress
2  using System.Net.Sockets;  // For TcpListener
3
4  class ThreadMain {
5
6    static void Main(string[] args) {
7
8      if (args.Length != 3)  // Test for correct # of args
9        throw new ArgumentException("Parameter(s): [<Optional properties>]"
10                            + " <Port> <Protocol> <Dispatcher>");
11
12     int servPort = Int32.Parse(args[0]);  // Server Port
13     String protocolName = args[1];         // Protocol name
14     String dispatcherName = args[2];       // Dispatcher name
15
16     TcpListener listener = new TcpListener(IPAddress.Any, servPort);
```

```
17      listener.Start();
18
19      ILogger logger = new ConsoleLogger();    // Log messages to console
20
21      System.Runtime.Remoting.ObjectHandle objHandle =
22                  Activator.CreateInstance(null, protocolName + "ProtocolFactory");
23      IProtocolFactory protoFactory = (IProtocolFactory)objHandle.Unwrap();
24
25      objHandle = Activator.CreateInstance(null, dispatcherName + "Dispatcher");
26      IDispatcher dispatcher = (IDispatcher)objHandle.Unwrap();
27
28      dispatcher.startDispatching(listener, logger, protoFactory);
29      /* NOT REACHED */
30   }
31 }
```

ThreadMain.cs

1. **Application setup and parameter parsing:** lines 8–14

2. **Create** TcpListener **and logger:** lines 16–19

3. **Instantiate a protocol factory:** lines 21–23
   The protocol name is passed as the second parameter. We adopt the naming convention of <ProtocolName>ProtocolFactory for the class name of the factory for the protocol name <ProtocolName>. For example, if the second parameter is "Echo," the corresponding protocol factory is EchoProtocolFactory. The static method Activator.CreateInstance() takes the name of a class and returns an Object-Handle object. The Unwrap() method of ObjectHandle creates a new instance of the class (casting to the proper type is required; in this case we use the IProtocol-Factory interface). *protoFactory* refers to this new instance of the specified protocol factory.

4. **Instantiate a dispatcher:** lines 25–26
   The dispatcher name is passed as the third parameter. We adopt the naming convention of <DispatcherType>Dispatcher for the class name of the dispatcher of type <DispatcherType>. For example, if the third parameter is "ThreadPer," the corresponding dispatcher is ThreadPerDispatcher. *dispatcher* refers to the new instance of the specified dispatcher.

5. **Start dispatching clients:** line 28

ThreadMain.cs makes it easy to use other protocols and dispatchers. The book's website (www.mkp.com/practical/csharpsockets) contains some additional examples.

4.4 Asynchronous I/O

The .NET framework provides a number of predefined network class methods that execute asynchronously. This allows code execution in the calling code to proceed while the I/O method waits to unblock. What's actually happening is that the asynchronous method is being executed in its own thread, except the details of setting up, data passing, and starting the thread are done for you. The calling code has three options to determine when the I/O call is completed: (1) it can specify a *callback* method to be invoked on completion; (2) it can *poll* periodically to see if the method has completed; or (3) after it has completed its asynchronous tasks, it can block waiting for completion.

The .NET framework is extremely flexible in how it provides asynchronous API capabilities. First, its library classes provide predefined nonblocking versions of methods for many different types of I/O, not just network calls. There are nonblocking versions of calls for network I/O, stream I/O, file I/O, even DNS lookups. Second, the .NET framework provides a mechanism for building an asynchronous version of any method, even user-defined methods. The latter is beyond the scope of this book, but in this section we will examine some of the existing asynchronous network methods.

An asynchronous I/O call is broken up into a *begin call* that is used to initiate the operation, and an *end call* that is used to retrieve the results of the call after it has completed. The begin call uses the same method name as the blocking version with the word Begin prepended to it. Likewise, the end call uses the same method name as the blocking version with the word End prepended to it. Begin and end operations are intended to be symmetrical, and each call to a begin method should be matched (at some point) with an end method call. Failure to do so in a long-running program creates an accumulation of state maintenance for the uncompleted asynchronous calls... in other words, a memory leak!

Let's look at some concrete examples. The NetworkStream class contains asynchronous versions of its Write() and Read() methods, implemented as BeginWrite(), EndWrite(), BeginRead(), and EndRead(). Let's take a look at these methods and examine how they relate to their blocking counterparts.

The BeginRead() and BeginWrite() methods take two additional arguments and have a different return type:

> **public override IAsyncResult** BeginRead(**byte**[] *buffer*, **int** *offset*, **int** *size*, **AsyncCallback** *callback*, **object** *state*);

> **public override IAsyncResult** BeginWrite(**byte**[] *buffer*, **int** *offset*, **int** *count*, **AsyncCallback** *callback*, **object** *state*);

The two additional arguments are an instance of AsyncCallback and an instance of object, which can be any C# class instance (predefined or user-defined). The AsyncCallback class is a *delegate* that specifies the callback method to invoke when the asynchronous option is complete. This class can be instantiated simply by passing it the name of the method for the callback:

```
AsyncCallback ac = new AsyncCallback(myMethodToCall);
⋮
public static void myMethodToCall(IAsyncResult result) {
   // callback code goes here
}
```

If no callback method is required, this argument can be null (although remember that the end method *must* be invoked somewhere). The callback method itself must have the signature `public static void <callbackMethodName>(IAsyncResult)`. The `IAsyncResult` class will be discussed in a moment.

The object argument is simply a way to convey user-defined information from the caller to the callback. This information could be the `NetworkStream` or socket class instance itself, or a user-defined class that includes both the `NetworkStream`, the byte buffer being used, and anything else to which the application callback method needs access.

The `BeginRead()` and `BeginWrite()` methods also have a different return type: an `IAsyncResult` instance. The `IAsyncResult` represents the status of the asynchronous operation and can be used to poll or block on the return of that operation. If you decide to block waiting for the operation to complete, the `IAsyncResult`'s `AsyncWaitHandle` property contains a method called `WaitOne()`. Invoking this method will block until the corresponding end method is called.

Once the asynchronous operation completes, the callback method is invoked. The callback method receives an `IAsyncResult` instance as an argument, which has a property called `AsyncState` that will contain an `object`. This object is the same object that was passed to the begin method, and needs to be cast to its original type before being used. The `IAsyncResult` instance is also used as the argument to the end call. The end call completes the symmetry of the call and returns the result of the call. That result is the exact same value that the synchronous version of the call would have returned.

public override int EndRead(**IAsyncResult** *asyncResult*);

public override void EndWrite(**IAsyncResult** *asyncResult*);

As an example let's assume that `BeginRead()` is called on a `NetworkStream` instance, and in addition to the usual arguments passed a callback method (new AsyncCall-back(myCallback)) and the read byte buffer as the state. The `EndRead()` call will return the number of bytes read from the `NetworkStream`, the same as a synchronous call to `Read()` would have.

```
public static void myCallback(IAsyncResult result) {
   byte[] buffer = (byte[])result.AsyncState;
   int bytesRead = EndRead(result);
   Console.WriteLine("Got {0} bytes of: {1}", bytesread, buffer);
}
```

Once you understand the differences between the synchronous and asynchronous versions of one method, the basic concepts can be extrapolated to cover the entire .NET asynchronous API. In summary, it involves:

1. **Begin Method:** The begin call takes (in addition to the arguments in the synchronous version of the method) an AsyncCallback instance specifying the callback method and an object containing any user-defined state. The begin call returns an IAsyncResult that can be used to poll or block on the call's return.

2. **Callback State:** The callback method is passed the state (the begin call's object argument) stored in the AsyncState property of the IAsyncResult instance.

3. **End Method:** The end method call takes as an argument the IAsyncResult instance returned by the callback invocation, and returns the value that the synchronous version of the call would have returned.

Figure 4.1 shows a pictorial depiction of how a BeginSend() call executes.

Table 4.2 lists some of the .NET classes used in this book that have asynchronous methods (this is not a complete list of all asynchronous methods .NET provides).

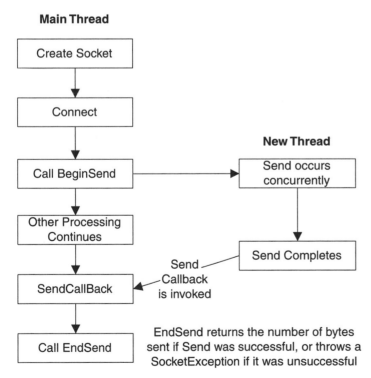

Figure 4.1: Asynchronous Send() example.

Class	Asynchronous Method API
Dns	BeginGetHostByName()/EndGetHostByName() BeginResolve()/EndResolve()
FileStream	BeginRead()/EndRead() BeginWrite()/EndWrite()
NetworkStream	BeginRead()/EndRead() BeginWrite()/EndWrite()
Socket	BeginAccept()/EndAccept() BeginConnect()/EndConnect() BeginReceive()/EndReceive() BeginReceiveFrom()/EndReceiveFrom() BeginSend()/EndSend() BeginSendTo()/EndSendTo()
Stream	BeginRead()/EndRead() BeginWrite()/EndWrite()

Table 4.2: Selected .NET Asynchronous Methods

Its time to look at some examples. Below we implement versions of TcpEchoClient and TcpEchoServer from Chapter 2 using the asynchronous API. The assumption in both cases is that the program has other operations it needs to be performing while blocking on the various network calls. To simulate that we added a simple doOtherStuff() method, which just loops five times, printing output and sleeping.

You will also note that the number of asynchronous methods defined for the Socket class is significantly more than what is defined for NetworkStream. In order to demonstrate the contrast between the two, the echo client uses the TcpClient class with a NetworkStream, and the echo server uses the Socket class.

TcpEchoClientAsync.cs

```
0  using System;              // For String, IAsyncResult, ArgumentException
1  using System.Text;         // For Encoding
2  using System.Net.Sockets;  // For TcpClient, NetworkStream
3  using System.Threading;    // For ManualResetEvent
4
5  class ClientState  {
6     // Object to contain client state, including the network stream
7     // and the send/recv buffer
```

```
8
9     private byte[] byteBuffer;
10    private NetworkStream netStream;
11    private StringBuilder echoResponse;
12    private int totalBytesRcvd = 0; // Total bytes received so far
13
14    public ClientState(NetworkStream netStream, byte[] byteBuffer) {
15      this.netStream = netStream;
16      this.byteBuffer = byteBuffer;
17      echoResponse = new StringBuilder();
18    }
19
20    public NetworkStream NetStream {
21      get {
22        return netStream;
23      }
24    }
25
26    public byte[] ByteBuffer {
27      set {
28        byteBuffer = value;
29      }
30      get {
31        return byteBuffer;
32      }
33    }
34
35    public void AppendResponse(String response) {
36      echoResponse.Append(response);
37    }
38    public String EchoResponse {
39      get {
40        return echoResponse.ToString();
41      }
42    }
43
44    public void AddToTotalBytes(int count) {
45      totalBytesRcvd += count;
46    }
47    public int TotalBytes {
48      get {
49        return totalBytesRcvd;
50      }
```

```
51     }
52   }
53
54   class TcpEchoClientAsync {
55
56     // A manual event signal we will trigger when all reads are complete:
57     public static ManualResetEvent ReadDone = new ManualResetEvent(false);
58
59     static void Main(string[] args) {
60
61       if ((args.Length < 2) || (args.Length > 3)) { // Test for correct # of args
62         throw new ArgumentException("Parameters: <Server> <Word> [<Port>]");
63       }
64
65       String server = args[0]; // Server name or IP address
66
67       // Use port argument if supplied, otherwise default to 7
68       int servPort = (args.Length == 3) ? Int32.Parse(args[2]) : 7;
69
70       Console.WriteLine("Thread {0} ({1}) - Main()",
71                         Thread.CurrentThread.GetHashCode(),
72                         Thread.CurrentThread.ThreadState);
73       // Create TcpClient that is connected to server on specified port
74       TcpClient client = new TcpClient();
75
76       client.Connect(server, servPort);
77       Console.WriteLine("Thread {0} ({1}) - Main(): connected to server",
78                         Thread.CurrentThread.GetHashCode(),
79                         Thread.CurrentThread.ThreadState);
80
81       NetworkStream netStream = client.GetStream();
82       ClientState cs = new ClientState(netStream,
83                                        Encoding.ASCII.GetBytes(args[1]));
84       // Send the encoded string to the server
85       IAsyncResult result = netStream.BeginWrite(cs.ByteBuffer, 0,
86                                                  cs.ByteBuffer.Length,
87                                                  new AsyncCallback(WriteCallback),
88                                                  cs);
89
90       doOtherStuff();
91
92       result.AsyncWaitHandle.WaitOne(); // block until EndWrite is called
93
```

```
94        // Receive the same string back from the server
95        result = netStream.BeginRead(cs.ByteBuffer, cs.TotalBytes,
96                              cs.ByteBuffer.Length - cs.TotalBytes,
97                              new AsyncCallback(ReadCallback), cs);
98
99      doOtherStuff();
100
101      ReadDone.WaitOne(); // Block until ReadDone is manually set
102
103      netStream.Close();  // Close the stream
104      client.Close();     // Close the socket
105    }
106
107    public static void doOtherStuff() {
108      for (int x=1; x<=5; x++) {
109        Console.WriteLine("Thread {0} ({1}) - doOtherStuff(): {2}...",
110                        Thread.CurrentThread.GetHashCode(),
111                        Thread.CurrentThread.ThreadState, x);
112      Thread.Sleep(1000);
113      }
114    }
115
116    public static void WriteCallback(IAsyncResult asyncResult) {
117
118      ClientState cs = (ClientState) asyncResult.AsyncState;
119
120      cs.NetStream.EndWrite(asyncResult);
121      Console.WriteLine("Thread {0} ({1}) - WriteCallback(): Sent {2} bytes...",
122                      Thread.CurrentThread.GetHashCode(),
123                      Thread.CurrentThread.ThreadState, cs.ByteBuffer.Length);
124    }
125
126    public static void ReadCallback(IAsyncResult asyncResult) {
127
128      ClientState cs = (ClientState) asyncResult.AsyncState;
129
130      int bytesRcvd = cs.NetStream.EndRead(asyncResult);
131
132      cs.AddToTotalBytes(bytesRcvd);
133      cs.AppendResponse(Encoding.ASCII.GetString(cs.ByteBuffer, 0, bytesRcvd));
134
135      if (cs.TotalBytes < cs.ByteBuffer.Length) {
136        Console.WriteLine("Thread {0} ({1}) - ReadCallback(): Received {2} bytes...",
```

```
137                        Thread.CurrentThread.GetHashCode(),
138                        Thread.CurrentThread.ThreadState, bytesRcvd);
139      cs.NetStream.BeginRead(cs.ByteBuffer, cs.TotalBytes,
140                        cs.ByteBuffer.Length - cs.TotalBytes,
141                        new AsyncCallback(ReadCallback), cs.NetStream);
142    } else {
143      Console.WriteLine("Thread {0} ({1}) - ReadCallback():
144                        Received {2} total " + "bytes: {3}",
145                        Thread.CurrentThread.GetHashCode(),
146                        Thread.CurrentThread.ThreadState, cs.TotalBytes,
147                        cs.EchoResponse);
148      ReadDone.Set(); // Signal read complete event
149    }
150  }
151 }
```

TcpEchoClientAsync.cs

1. ClientState **class:** lines 5–52
   The ClientState class is used to store the send/receive buffer, NetworkStream, the echo response, and a total byte count. It is used to pass state to the callback methods.

2. **Argument parsing:** lines 61–68

3. **Print state,** TcpClient **creation and setup:** lines 70–79
   Create a TcpClient instance and connect to the remote server.

4. **Store state in** ClientState **instance:** lines 81–82
   Create a ClientState instance and store the network stream and command-line input bytes to be sent.

5. **Call** BeginWrite**:** lines 84–88
   Call BeginWrite() with the standard Write() arguments plus a user-defined callback method of WriteCallback() (wrapped in an AsyncCallback delegate instance) and a state object reference to the user-defined ClientState.

6. **Perform asynchronous processing, then block:** lines 90–92
   Call doOtherStuff() to simulate asynchronous processing, then use the AsyncWaitHandle property of the IAsyncResult to call WaitOne(), which blocks until EndWrite() is called.

7. **Call** BeginRead**:** lines 94–97
   Call BeginRead() with the standard Read() arguments plus a user-defined callback method of ReadCallback() (wrapped in an AsyncCallback delegate instance) and a state object reference to the user-defined ClientState.

8. **Perform asynchronous processing, then block:** lines 99–101
   Call doOtherStuff() to simulate asynchronous processing, then use the Manual-ResetEvent class instance *ReadDone* to call WaitOne(), which blocks until *Read-Done()* has been set. Note that we cannot use the IAsyncResult from the BeginRead() in this case, because that would unblock us after the first read, and we may have multiple reads.

9. **Close the stream and socket:** lines 103–104

10. doOtherStuff()**:** lines 107–114
    Simulate other processing by writing some output in a loop with Thread.Sleep() prolonging the intervals slightly.

11. WriteCallback()**:** lines 116–124
    - **Retrieve the state object:** lines 118
      The write callback state object was a ClientState instance, so store it as a local variable by casting the IAsyncResult instance property AsyncState as a ClientState.
    - **EndWrite():** line 120
      Call the EndWrite() method to complete the operation.
    - **Output the number of bytes sent:** lines 121–123

12. ReadCallback()**:** lines 126–150
    - **Retrieve the state object:** lines 128–130
      The read callback state object was a ClientState instance, so store it as a local variable by casting the IAsyncResult instance property AsyncState as a ClientState. Create local variables where convenient.
    - **Issue another** BeginRead()**:** lines 135–142
      If the length of the response is less than the expected response, issue another BeginRead() to get the remaining bytes.
    - **Output the echo response:** lines 143–148
      If all bytes have been received, output the echo response.
    - **Trigger** ManualResetEvent**:** line 149
      Manually trigger the *ReadDone* ManualResetEvent so we can unblock if we are blocking on read completion.

TcpEchoServerAsync.cs

```
0  using System;         // For Console, IAsyncResult, ArgumentException
1  using System.Net;     // For IPEndPoint
```

```
2  using System.Net.Sockets;   // For Socket
3  using System.Threading;      // For ManualResetEvent
4
5  class ClientState {
6    // Object to contain client state, including the client socket
7    // and the receive buffer
8
9    private const int BUFSIZE = 32; // Size of receive buffer
10   private byte[] rcvBuffer;
11   private Socket clntSock;
12
13   public ClientState(Socket clntSock) {
14     this.clntSock = clntSock;
15     rcvBuffer = new byte[BUFSIZE]; // Receive buffer
16   }
17
18   public byte[] RcvBuffer {
19     get {
20       return rcvBuffer;
21     }
22   }
23
24   public Socket ClntSock {
25     get {
26       return clntSock;
27     }
28   }
29  }
30
31  class TcpEchoServerAsync {
32
33    private const int BACKLOG = 5;   // Outstanding connection queue max size
34
35    static void Main(string[] args) {
36
37      if (args.Length != 1) // Test for correct # of args
38        throw new ArgumentException("Parameters: <Port>");
39
40      int servPort = Int32.Parse(args[0]);
41
42      // Create a Socket to accept client connections
43      Socket servSock = new Socket(AddressFamily.InterNetwork, SocketType.Stream,
44                                   ProtocolType.Tcp);
```

```
45
46      servSock.Bind(new IPEndPoint(IPAddress.Any, servPort));
47      servSock.Listen(BACKLOG);
48
49      for (;;) { // Run forever, accepting and servicing connections
50        Console.WriteLine("Thread {0} ({1}) - Main(): calling BeginAccept()",
51                          Thread.CurrentThread.GetHashCode(),
52                          Thread.CurrentThread.ThreadState);
53
54        IAsyncResult result = servSock.BeginAccept(new AsyncCallback(AcceptCallback),
55                                                   servSock);
56        doOtherStuff();
57
58        // Wait for the EndAccept before issuing a new BeginAccept
59        result.AsyncWaitHandle.WaitOne();
60      }
61    }
62
63    public static void doOtherStuff() {
64      for (int x=1; x<=5; x++) {
65        Console.WriteLine("Thread {0} ({1}) - doOtherStuff(): {2}...",
66                          Thread.CurrentThread.GetHashCode(),
67                          Thread.CurrentThread.ThreadState, x);
68      Thread.Sleep(1000);
69      }
70    }
71
72    public static void AcceptCallback(IAsyncResult asyncResult) {
73
74      Socket servSock = (Socket) asyncResult.AsyncState;
75      Socket clntSock = null;
76
77      try {
78
79        clntSock = servSock.EndAccept(asyncResult);
80
81        Console.WriteLine("Thread {0} ({1}) - AcceptCallback(): handling client at {2}",
82                          Thread.CurrentThread.GetHashCode(),
83                          Thread.CurrentThread.ThreadState,
84                          clntSock.RemoteEndPoint);
85
86        ClientState cs = new ClientState(clntSock);
87
```

```
88           clntSock.BeginReceive(cs.RcvBuffer, 0, cs.RcvBuffer.Length, SocketFlags.None,
89                             new AsyncCallback(ReceiveCallback), cs);
90      } catch (SocketException se) {
91       Console.WriteLine(se.ErrorCode + ": " + se.Message);
92       clntSock.Close();
93      }
94  }
95
96  public static void ReceiveCallback(IAsyncResult asyncResult) {
97
98    ClientState cs = (ClientState) asyncResult.AsyncState;
99
100   try {
101
102     int recvMsgSize = cs.ClntSock.EndReceive(asyncResult);
103
104     if (recvMsgSize > 0) {
105       Console.WriteLine("Thread {0} ({1}) - ReceiveCallback(): received {2} bytes",
106                       Thread.CurrentThread.GetHashCode(),
107                       Thread.CurrentThread.ThreadState,
108                       recvMsgSize);
109
110       cs.ClntSock.BeginSend(cs.RcvBuffer, 0, recvMsgSize, SocketFlags.None,
111                         new AsyncCallback(SendCallback), cs);
112     } else {
113       cs.ClntSock.Close();
114     }
115   } catch (SocketException se) {
116     Console.WriteLine(se.ErrorCode + ": " + se.Message);
117     cs.ClntSock.Close();
118   }
119 }
120
121 public static void SendCallback(IAsyncResult asyncResult) {
122   ClientState cs = (ClientState) asyncResult.AsyncState;
123
124   try {
125
126     int bytesSent = cs.ClntSock.EndSend(asyncResult);
127
128     Console.WriteLine("Thread {0} ({1}) - SendCallback(): sent {2} bytes",
129                       Thread.CurrentThread.GetHashCode(),
```

```
130                      Thread.CurrentThread.ThreadState,
131                      bytesSent);
132
133        cs.ClntSock.BeginReceive(cs.RcvBuffer, 0, cs.RcvBuffer.Length,
134                    SocketFlags.None, new AsyncCallback(ReceiveCallback), cs);
135      } catch (SocketException se) {
136        Console.WriteLine(se.ErrorCode + ": " + se.Message);
137        cs.ClntSock.Close();
138      }
139    }
140  }
```

TcpEchoServerAsync.cs

1. ClientState **class:** lines 5–29
   The ClientState class is used to store the receive buffer and client Socket, and is used to pass state to the callback methods.

2. **Argument parsing:** lines 37–40
   The server port is the only argument.

3. **Socket creation and setup:** lines 42–47
   Bind and listen on the newly created socket.

4. **Main loop**: lines 49–60
   Loop forever performing:

   ■ **Output current thread information:** lines 50–52
   Include the thread number by calling Thread.CurrentThread.GetHashCode() and the thread state (running or background) by accessing the property Thread.CurrentThread.ThreadState.

   ■ **Asynchronous accept call:** lines 54–55
   Call BeginAccept() with a user-defined callback method of AcceptCallback() (wrapped in an AsyncCallback delegate instance) and a state object reference to the server Socket. Store the returned IAsyncResult so we can block on it later.

   ■ **Perform other processing:** line 56
   Call the method doOtherStuff() to continue main code execution asynchronously.

   ■ **Block waiting for the accept to complete:** lines 58–59
   Once we have finished our asynchronous processing, we don't want to call accept an indefinite amount of times if nothing is happening. Wait until the End-Accept() call is executed by calling the WaitOne() method on the IAsyncResult's AsyncWaitHandle.

5. `doOtherStuff()`: lines 63–70
Simulate other processing by writing some output in a loop with `Thread.Sleep()` prolonging the intervals slightly.

6. `AcceptCallback()`: lines 72–94

■ **Retrieve the state object:** line 74
The accept callback state object was the server socket, so store the server socket as a local variable by casting the `IAsyncResult` instance property `AsyncState` as a `Socket`.

■ **Call** `EndAccept()`: line 79
The `EndAccept()` call returns the client `Socket` instance.

■ **Output the thread state and client connection:** lines 81–84
Output the thread number and state and the client that we have connected.

■ **Create a** `ClientState` **instance:** line 86
In preparation for calling our next asynchronous method, instantiate our user-defined state object.

■ **Call** `BeginReceive()`: lines 88–89
Call BeginReceive() with the standard Receive() arguments, plus a user-defined callback method of ReceiveCallback() (wrapped in an AsyncCallback delegate instance) and a state object reference to the user-defined ClientState.

■ **Catch exceptions:** lines 90–92
Since a server should be robust, catch any exceptions that occur on this client connection, and close the client socket and continue if they occur.

7. `ReceiveCallback()`: lines 96–119

■ **Retrieve the state object:** lines 98
The receive callback state object was the ClientState instance, so store it as a local variable by casting the `IAsyncResult` instance property `AsyncState` as a `ClientState`.

■ **Call** `EndReceive()`: line 102
The `EndReceive()` call returns the bytes received.

■ **Output the bytes received:** lines 105–108
If the bytes received were greater than zero, output the bytes returned to the console. If the bytes received is equal to zero, we are done, so close the client socket and drop out of the method.

■ **Call** `BeginSend()`: lines 110–111
Call BeginSend() with the standard Send() arguments plus a user-defined callback method of SendCallback() (wrapped in an AsyncCallback delegate instance) and a state object reference to the user-defined ClientState.

■ **Catch exceptions:** lines 115–118
Since a server should be robust, catch any exceptions that occur on this client connection, and close the client socket and continue if they occur.

8. SendCallback(): lines 121–139
   - **Retrieve the state object:** lines 122
     The send callback state object was the ClientState instance, so store it as a local variable by casting the IAsyncResult instance property AsyncState as a ClientState.
   - **Call** EndSend(): line 126
     The EndSend() call returns the bytes sent.
   - **Output the bytes sent:** lines 128–131
     Output the number of bytes sent to the console.
   - **Call** BeginReceive(): lines 133–134
     Since there may be more bytes to receive (until we get a bytes received value of zero), recursively call BeginReceive() again. The arguments are the same—the Receive() arguments plus a user-defined callback method of SendCallback() (wrapped in an AsyncCallback delegate instance) and a state object reference to the user-defined ClientState.
   - **Catch exceptions:** lines 135–138
     Since a server should be robust, catch any exceptions that occur on this client connection, and close the client socket and continue if they occur.

A final option for handling asynchronous call completion is *polling*. As we have seen, polling involves having the main thread periodically check in with the asynchronous operation to see if it is completed. This can be achieved with the IsCompleted property of the IAsyncResult class:

```
    :
IAsyncResult result = netStream.BeginRead(buffer, 0, buffer.Length,
                                new AsyncCallback(myMethod),
                                myStateObject);
for (;;) {
   if (result.isCompleted) {
     // handle read here
   }
   // do other work here
   :
}
```

As mentioned earlier, polling is typically not very efficient. Callbacks are usually the preferred method of handling asynchronous method completion.

4.5 Multiple Recipients

So far all of our sockets have dealt with communication between exactly two entities, usually a server and a client. Such one-to-one communication is sometimes called *unicast*.

Some information is of interest to multiple recipients. In such cases, we could unicast a copy of the data to each recipient, but this may be very inefficient. Unicasting multiple copies over a single network connection wastes bandwidth by sending the same information multiple times. In fact, if we want to send data at a fixed rate, the bandwidth of our network connection defines a hard limit on the number of receivers we can support. For example, if our video server sends 1Mbps streams and its network connection is only 3Mbps (a healthy connection rate), we can only support three simultaneous users.

Fortunately, networks provide a way to use bandwidth more efficiently. Instead of making the sender responsible for duplicating packets, we can give this job to the network. In our video server example, we send a single copy of the stream across the server's connection to the network, which then duplicates the data only when appropriate. With this model of duplication, the server uses only 1Mbps across its connection to the network, irrespective of the number of clients.

There are two types of one-to-many service: *broadcast* and *multicast*. With broadcast, all hosts on the (local) network receive a copy of the message. With multicast, the message is sent to a *multicast address*, and the network delivers it only to those hosts that have indicated that they want to receive messages sent to that address. In general, only UDP sockets are allowed to broadcast or multicast.

4.5.1 Broadcast

Broadcasting UDP datagrams is similar to unicasting datagrams, except that a *broadcast address* is used instead of a regular (unicast) IP address. The *local broadcast* address (255.255.255.255) sends the message to every host on the same broadcast network. Local broadcast messages are never forwarded by routers. A host on an Ethernet network can send a message to all other hosts on that same Ethernet, but the message will not be forwarded by a router. IP also specifies *directed broadcast* addresses, which allow broadcasts to all hosts on a specified network; however, since most Internet routers do not forward directed broadcasts, we do not deal with them here.

There is no networkwide broadcast address that can be used to send a message to all hosts. To see why, consider the impact of a broadcast to every host on the Internet. Sending a single datagram would result in a very, very large number of packet duplications by the routers, and bandwidth would be consumed on each and every network. The consequences of misuse (malicious or accidental) are too great, so the designers of IP left such an Internet-wide broadcast facility out on purpose.

Even so, local broadcast can be very useful. Often, it is used in state exchange for network games where the players are all on the same local (broadcast) network. In C#, the code for unicasting and broadcasting is the same. To play with broadcasting applications, simply run SendUdp.cs using a broadcast destination address.[2] Run RecvUdp.cs as you did before (except that you can run several receivers at one time).

---

[2]Note that some operating systems require setting SocketOptionName.Broadcast to true before broadcasting is allowed, or an exception will be thrown. This is most likely if you are running .NET on a UNIX-based machine using Mono.

4.5.2 Multicast

As with broadcast, the main difference between multicast and unicast is the form of the address. A multicast address identifies a set of receivers. The designers of IP allocated a range of the address space (from 224.0.0.0 to 239.255.255.255) dedicated to multicast. With the exception of a few reserved multicast addresses, a sender can send datagrams addressed to any address in this range. In C#, multicast applications generally communicate using an instance of Socket or UdpClient. It is important to understand that a multicast socket is actually a UDP socket with some extra multicast-specific attributes that can be controlled. Our next example implements the multicast version of SendUdp.cs (see page 82). First we show the code for the helper class MCIPAddress.cs, which allows us to validate multicast IP addresses.

MCIPAddress.cs

```
0   using System;        // For String
1
2   public class MCIPAddress {
3     public static Boolean isValid(String ip) {
4       try {
5         int octet1 = Int32.Parse(ip.Split(new Char[]{'.'}, 4)[0]);
6         if ((octet1 >= 224) && (octet1 <= 239)) return true;
7       } catch (Exception) {}
8       return false;
9     }
10  }
```

MCIPAddress.cs

The MCIPAddress class has a static isValid() method that simply validates that the string dotted-quad notation IP passed to it is in the valid range. We simply isolate the first octet of the IP address, convert it to an integer, and validate its value.

SendUDPMulticast.cs

```
0   using System;              // For Int32, ArgumentException
1   using System.Net;          // For IPAddress, IPEndpoint
2   using System.Net.Sockets;  // For Socket and associated classes
3
4   public class SendUdpMulticast {
5
6     public static void Main(string[] args) {
7
```

```
8     if ((args.Length < 2) || (args.Length > 3)) // Test for correct # of args
9       throw new ArgumentException(
10         "Parameter(s): <Multicast Addr> <Port> [<TTL>]");
11
12    IPAddress destAddr = IPAddress.Parse(args[0]);  // Destination address
13
14    if (! MCIPAddress.isValid(args[0]))
15      throw new ArgumentException("Valid MC addr: 224.0.0.0 - 239.255.255.255");
16
17    int destPort = Int32.Parse(args[1]);  // Destination port
18
19    int TTL;   // Time to live for datagram
20    if (args.Length == 3)
21      TTL = Int32.Parse(args[2]);
22    else
23      TTL = 1;  // Default TTL
24
25    ItemQuote quote = new ItemQuote(1234567890987654L, "5mm Super Widgets",
26                                    1000, 12999, true, false);
27
28    Socket sock = new Socket(AddressFamily.InterNetwork,
29                             SocketType.Dgram,
30                             ProtocolType.Udp ); // Multicast socket to sending
31
32    // Set the Time to Live
33    sock.SetSocketOption(SocketOptionLevel.IP,
34                         SocketOptionName.MulticastTimeToLive,
35                         TTL);
36
37    ItemQuoteEncoderText encoder = new ItemQuoteEncoderText();  // Text encoding
38    byte[] codedQuote = encoder.encode(quote);
39
40    // Create an IP endpoint class instance
41    IPEndPoint ipep = new IPEndPoint(destAddr, destPort);
42
43    // Create and send a packet
44    sock.SendTo(codedQuote, 0, codedQuote.Length, SocketFlags.None, ipep);
45
46    sock.Close();
47  }
48 }
```

SendUDPMulticast.cs

The only significant differences between our unicast and multicast senders are that (1) we verify that the given address is multicast, and (2) we set the initial Time To Live (TTL) value for the multicast datagram. Every IP datagram contains a TTL, initialized to some default value and decremented (usually by one) by each router that forwards the packet. When the TTL reaches zero, the packet is discarded. By setting the initial value of the TTL, we limit the distance that a packet can travel from the sender.[3] For the Socket class the TTL is set using the SetSocketOption() method with the SocketOption-Name.MulticastTimeToLive option. The UdpClient class can set the TTL by calling the JoinMulticastGroup() method with the optional TTL argument (this is a slightly odd API, since joining multicast groups is really only required for receiving, not sending).

Unlike broadcast, where receivers don't have to do anything special to receive broadcast packets, with multicast the network delivers the message only to a specific set of hosts, namely those that have indicated a desire to receive them. This set of receivers, called a *multicast group*, is identified by a shared multicast (or group) address. Receivers need some mechanism to notify the network of their interest in receiving data sent to a particular multicast address, so that the network can forward packets to them. This notification is called *joining a group* or *adding a membership*. To stop packets from a group being delivered, a corresponding notification to leave the group or *drop the membership* is sent. Closing a socket implicitly causes joined groups to be left (provided no other socket is still a member of the group). The group notifications are accomplished with the Socket class by using the SetSocketOption() method with the SocketOptionName.AddMembership and SocketOptionName.DropMembership options. The argument to the SetSocketOption() method is an instance of MulticastOption, which contains the IP address of the multicast group to add or drop. The UdpClient class can join multicast groups using the Join-MulticastGroup() method and drop them with the DropMulticastGroup() method. Our multicast receiver joins a specified group, receives and prints a single multicast message from that group, leaves the group, and exits.

RecvUdpMulticast.cs

```
0   using System;                // For Console, Int32, ArgumentException
1   using System.Net;            // For IPAddress, EndPoinit, IPEndPoint
2   using System.Net.Sockets;    // For Socket and associated classes
3
4   public class RecvUdpMulticast {
5
6       public static void Main(string[] args) {
```

---

[3]The rules for multicast TTL are actually not quite so simple. It is not necessarily the case that a packet with TTL = 4 can travel four hops from the sender; however, it will not travel *more* than four hops.

```
7
8    if (args.Length != 2)   // Test for correct # of args
9      throw new ArgumentException("Parameter(s): <Multicast Addr> <Port>");
10
11   IPAddress address = IPAddress.Parse(args[0]);   // Multicast address
12
13   if (! MCIPAddress.isValid(args[0]))
14     throw new ArgumentException("Valid MC addr: 224.0.0.0 - 239.255.255.255");
15
16   int port = Int32.Parse(args[1]);   // Multicast port
17
18   Socket sock = new Socket(AddressFamily.InterNetwork, SocketType.Dgram,
19                            ProtocolType.Udp); // Multicast receiving socket
20
21   // Set the reuse address option
22   sock.SetSocketOption(SocketOptionLevel.Socket,
23                        SocketOptionName.ReuseAddress, 1);
24
25   // Create an IPEndPoint and bind to it
26   IPEndPoint ipep = new IPEndPoint(IPAddress.Any, port);
27   sock.Bind(ipep);
28
29   // Add membership in the multicast group
30   sock.SetSocketOption(SocketOptionLevel.IP,
31                        SocketOptionName.AddMembership,
32                        new MulticastOption(address, IPAddress.Any));
33
34   IPEndPoint receivePoint = new IPEndPoint(IPAddress.Any, 0);
35   EndPoint tempReceivePoint = (EndPoint)receivePoint;
36
37   // Create and receive a datagram
38   byte[] packet = new byte[ItemQuoteTextConst.MAX_WIRE_LENGTH];
39   int length = sock.ReceiveFrom(packet, 0, ItemQuoteTextConst.MAX_WIRE_LENGTH,
40                        SocketFlags.None, ref tempReceivePoint);
41
42   ItemQuoteDecoderText decoder = new ItemQuoteDecoderText();   // Text decoding
43   ItemQuote quote = decoder.decode(packet);
44   Console.WriteLine(quote);
45
46   // Drop membership in the multicast group
47   sock.SetSocketOption(SocketOptionLevel.IP,
48                        SocketOptionName.DropMembership,
49                        new MulticastOption(address, IPAddress.Any));
```

```
50      sock.Close();
51    }
52  }
```

RecvUdpMulticast.cs

The two significant differences between our multicast and unicast receivers is that the multicast receiver must join the multicast group by supplying the desired multicast address and set the address reuse option. The setting of the address reuse option is optional, but without it you will be unable to have two simultaneous multicast receivers on the same host.

Multicast datagrams can, in fact, be sent from a Socket or UdpClient by simply using a multicast address. In this case the TTL defaults to 1. You can test this by using SendUdp.cs (see page 82) to send to the multicast receiver. A multicast receiver, on the other hand, *must* use multicast-specific code in order to join the multicast group.

The decision to use broadcast or multicast depends on several factors, including the network location of receivers and the knowledge of the communicating parties. The scope of a broadcast on the Internet is restricted to a local broadcast network, placing severe restrictions on the location of the broadcast receivers. Multicast communication may include receivers anywhere in the network,[4] so multicast has the advantage that it can cover a distributed set of receivers. The disadvantage of IP multicast is that receivers must know the address of a multicast group to join. Knowledge of an address is not required to receive broadcast. In some contexts, this makes broadcast a better mechanism than multicast for discovery. All hosts can receive broadcast by default, so it is simple to ask all hosts on a single network a question like "Where's the printer?"

UDP unicast, multicast, and broadcast are all implemented using an underlying UDP socket. The semantics of most implementations are such that a UDP datagram will be delivered to all sockets bound to the destination port of the packet. That is, a UDP Socket or UdpClient instance bound to a local port X (with local address not specified, i.e., an IPAddress.Any wild card), on a host with address Y will receive any UDP datagram destined for port X that is (1) unicast with destination address Y, (2) multicast to a group that *any* application on Y has joined, or (3) broadcast where it can reach host Y. A receiver can use Connect() to limit the datagram source address and port. Also, a unicast UDP socket instance can specify the local unicast address, which prevents delivery of multicast and broadcast packets. See Section 5.5 for details on datagram demultiplexing. For more details on implementing multicast applications, see the *Multicast Sockets* book in the Practical Guide series [26].

---

[4]At the time of writing of this book, there are severe limitations on who can receive multicast traffic on the Internet; however, multicast availability should improve over time. Multicast should work if the sender and receivers are on the same LAN segment.

4.6 Closing Connections

You've probably never given much thought to who closes a connection. In phone conversations, either side can start the process of terminating the call. It typically goes something like this:

"Well, I guess I'd better go."

"OK. Bye."

"Bye."

Network protocols, on the other hand, are typically very specific about who "closes" first. In the echo protocol, Figure 4.2(a), the server dutifully echoes everything the client sends. When the client is finished, it calls Close(). After the server has received and echoed all of the data sent before the client's call to Close(), its read operation returns a 0, indicating that the client is finished. The server then calls Close() on its socket. The close is a critical part of the protocol because without it the server doesn't know when the client is finished sending characters to echo. In HTTP, Figure 4.2(b), it's the server that initiates the connection close. Here, the client sends a request ("GET") to the server, and the server responds by sending a header (normally starting with "200 OK"), followed by the requested file. Since the client does not know the size of the file, the server must indicate the end-of-file by closing the socket.[5]

Calling Close() on a Socket terminates *both* directions (input and output) of data flow. (Section 5.4.2 provides a more detailed description of TCP connection termination.) Once an endpoint (client or server) closes the socket, it can no longer send *or receive* data. This means that Close() can only be used to signal the other end when the caller is completely finished communicating. In the echo protocol, once the server receives the

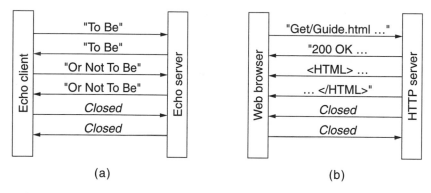

(a)   (b)

Figure 4.2: Echo (a) and HTTP (b) protocol termination.

---

[5]Note that HTTP does provide an application-level mechanism to determine the end of file, the Content-Length header field, but this header is not required on an HTTP response. A robust client should be prepared to handle responses without it.

close from the client, it immediately closes. In effect, the client close indicates that the communication is completed. Basic HTTP works the same way, except that the server is the terminator.[6]

Let's consider a different protocol. Suppose you want a transcoding server that takes a stream of bytes in Unicode, converts them to UTF-8, and sends the UTF-8 stream back to the client. Which endpoint should close the connection? Since the stream of bytes from the client is arbitrarily long, the client needs to close the connection so that the server knows when the stream of bytes to be encoded ends. When should the client call Close()? If the client calls Close() on the socket immediately after it sends the last byte of data, it will not be able to receive the last bytes of UTF-8 data. Perhaps the client could wait until it receives all of the UTF-8 data before it closes, as the echo protocol does. Unfortunately, neither the server nor the client knows how many bytes to expect since UTF-8 encoding is of variable length (see Section 3.1.1), so this will not work either. What is needed is a way to tell the other end of the connection "I am through sending," without losing the ability to receive.

Fortunately, sockets provide a way to do this. The Shutdown() method of Socket allows the I/O streams to be closed independently. The Shutdown() method takes as an argument an instance of the SocketShutdown enumeration, which can have the values Send, Receive, or Both. After a call to Shutdown(SocketShutdown.Receive), the socket can no longer receive input. Any undelivered data is silently discarded, and any attempt to read from the socket will generate a SocketException. After Shutdown(SocketShutdown.Send) is called on a Socket, no more data may be sent on the socket. Attempts to write to the stream also throw a SocketException. Any data written before the call to Shutdown(SocketShutdown.Send) may be read by the remote socket. After this, a read on the input stream of the remote socket will return 0. An application calling Shutdown(SocketShutdown.Send) can continue to read from the socket and, similarly, data can be written after calling Shutdown(SocketShutdown.Receive).

In the Transcode protocol (see Figure 4.3), the client writes the Unicode bytes, closing the output stream using Shutdown(SocketShutdown.Send) when finished sending, and reads the UTF-8 byte stream from the server. The server repeatedly reads the Unicode data and writes the UTF-8 data until the client performs a shutdown, causing the server read to return 0, indicating an end-of-stream. The server then closes the connection and exits. After the client calls Shutdown(SocketShutdown.Send), it needs to read any remaining UTF-8 bytes from the server.

Our client, TranscodeClient.cs, implements the client side of the Transcode protocol. The Unicode bytes are read from the file specified on the command line, and the UTF-8 bytes are written to a new file. If the Unicode filename is "data," the UTF-8 file name is "data.ut8." Note that this implementation works for small files, but that there is a flaw that causes deadlock for large files. (We discuss and correct this shortcoming in Section 5.2.)

---

[6]More sophisticated features of HTTP, such as persistent connections, are quite common today and operate differently.

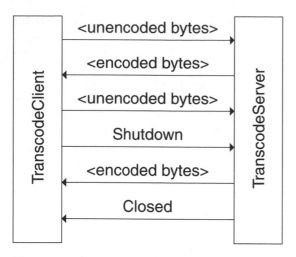

Figure 4.3: Transcode Server protocol termination.

As we mentioned earlier, some advanced functionality is available only in the Socket class and not the higher level socket classes like TcpClient. The Shutdown() method of the Socket class is an example of a feature that is not directly accessible in the TcpClient class. However, the TcpClient class does give us access to its underlying Socket instance through its protected Socket property. Since the property is protected, it can only be accessed by extending the original TcpClient class. We have decided to illustrate this technique here by extending the TcpClient class to access the Socket method Shutdown(). We have created the TcpClientShutdown class in order to do this.

TcpClientShutdown.cs

```
0   using System;             // For String
1   using System.Net;         // For IPEndPoint, EndPoint
2   using System.Net.Sockets; // For TcpClient, SocketShutdown
3
4   class TcpClientShutdown : TcpClient {
5
6     public TcpClientShutdown():base() {}
7     public TcpClientShutdown(IPEndPoint localEP):base(localEP) {}
8     public TcpClientShutdown(String server, int port):base(server, port) {}
9
10    public void Shutdown(SocketShutdown ss) {
11      // Invoke the Shutdown method on the underlying socket
12      this.Client.Shutdown(ss);
13    }
```

```
14    public EndPoint GetRemoteEndPoint() {
15      // Return the RemoteEndPoint from the underlying socket
16      return this.Client.RemoteEndPoint;
17    }
18  }
```

1. **Extend the** TcpClient **class:** line 4

2. **Extend the constructors:** lines 6–8
   Extending the constructors with the base keyword is required. Additional constructor logic can also be added but is not required.

3. Shutdown()**:** lines 10–13
   The new user-defined Shutdown() method invokes the Socket method of the same name by using the Client property.

4. GetRemoteEndPoint()**:** lines 14–17
   The new user-defined GetRemoteEndPoint() method retrieves the RemoteEndPoint property from the underlying Socket by using the Client property.

TranscodeClient.cs

```
0  using System;           // For String, Int32, Console, ArgumentException
1  using System.IO;        // For FileStream
2  using System.Net.Sockets; // For NetworkStream, TcpClient
3
4  public class TranscodeClient {
5
6    private const int BUFSIZE = 256;  // Size of read buffer
7
8    private static NetworkStream netStream;
9    private static FileStream fileIn;
10   private static TcpClientShutdown client;
11
12   public static void Main(string[] args) {
13
14     if (args.Length != 3)  // Test for correct # of args
15       throw new ArgumentException("Parameter(s): <Server> <Port> <File>");
16
17     String server = args[0];        // Server name or IP address
18     int port = Int32.Parse(args[1]); // Server port
19     String filename = args[2];      // File to read data from
```

```
20
21     // Open input and output file (named <input>.ut8)
22     fileIn = new FileStream(filename, FileMode.Open, FileAccess.Read);
23     FileStream fileOut = new FileStream(filename + ".ut8", FileMode.Create);
24
25     // Create TcpClient connected to server on specified port
26     client = new TcpClientShutdown();
27     client.Connect(server, port);
28
29     // Send nonencoded byte stream to server
30     netStream = client.GetStream();
31     sendBytes();
32
33     // Receive encoded byte stream from server
34     int bytesRead;                          // Number of bytes read
35     byte[] buffer = new byte[BUFSIZE];   // Byte buffer
36     while ((bytesRead = netStream.Read(buffer, 0, buffer.Length)) > 0) {
37       fileOut.Write(buffer, 0, bytesRead);
38       Console.Write("R");    // Reading progress indicator
39     }
40
41     Console.WriteLine(); // End progress indicator line
42
43     netStream.Close(); // Close the stream
44     client.Close();    // Close the socket
45     fileIn.Close();    // Close input file
46     fileOut.Close();   // Close output file
47   }
48
49   private static void sendBytes() {
50     int bytesRead;                          // Number of bytes read
51     BufferedStream fileInBuf = new BufferedStream(fileIn);
52     byte[] buffer = new byte[BUFSIZE];   // Byte buffer
53     while ((bytesRead = fileInBuf.Read(buffer, 0, buffer.Length)) > 0) {
54       netStream.Write(buffer, 0, bytesRead);
55       Console.Write("W");    // Writing progress indicator
56     }
57     client.Shutdown(SocketShutdown.Send);     // Done sending
58   }
59 }
```

1. **Application setup and parameter parsing:** lines 14–19

2. **Create socket and open files:** lines 21–30
   Using the TcpClientShutdown class to allow us access to the underlying Socket methods and properties.

3. **Invoke** sendBytes() **to transmit bytes:** line 31

4. **Receive the UTF-8 data stream:** lines 33–39
   The while loop receives the UTF-8 data stream and writes the bytes to the output file until an end-of-stream is signaled by a 0 from Read().

5. **Close socket and streams:** lines 43–46

6. sendBytes()**:** lines 49–58
   Given a socket connected to a Transcode server and the file input stream, read all of the Unicode bytes from the file and write them to the socket network stream.

   ■ **Set up input file buffered stream:** lines 50–52

   ■ **Send Unicode bytes to Transcode server:** lines 53–56
     The while loop reads from the input stream (in this case from a buffered file stream) and repeats the bytes to the socket network stream until end-of-file, indicated by 0 from Read(). Each write is indicated by a "W" printed to the console.

   ■ **Shut down the socket output stream:** line 57
     After reading and sending all of the bytes from the input file, shut down the output stream, notifying the server that the client is finished sending. The close will cause a 0 return from Read() on the server.

   To implement the Transcode server, we simply write a server-side conversion protocol using the static UTF-8 Encoding class. The server receives the Unicode bytes from the client, converts them to UTF-8, and writes them back to the client.

TranscodeServer.cs

```
0  using System;              // For String, Int32, Console
1  using System.Text;         // For Encoding
2  using System.Net;          // For IPAddress
3  using System.Net.Sockets;  // For TcpListener, TcpClient, NetworkStream
4
5  public class TranscodeServer {
6
7    public static readonly int BUFSIZE = 1024;   // Size of read buffer
8
9    public static void Main(string[] args) {
10
11     if (args.Length != 1)  // Test for correct # of args
12       throw new ArgumentException("Parameter(s): <Port>");
```

```
13
14      int servPort = Int32.Parse(args[0]);   // Server port
15
16      // Create a TcpListener to accept client connection requests
17      TcpListener listener = new TcpListener(IPAddress.Any, servPort);
18      listener.Start();
19
20      byte[] buffer = new byte[BUFSIZE];     // Allocate read/write buffer
21      int bytesRead;                         // Number of bytes read
22      for (;;) { // Run forever, accepting and servicing connections
23        // Wait for client to connect, then create a new TcpClient
24        TcpClient client = listener.AcceptTcpClient();
25
26        Console.WriteLine("\nHandling client...");
27
28        // Get the input and output streams from socket
29        NetworkStream netStream = client.GetStream();
30
31        int totalBytesRead = 0;
32        int totalBytesWritten = 0;
33
34        Decoder uniDecoder = Encoding.Unicode.GetDecoder();
35        Char[] chars = null;
36
37        // Receive until client closes connection, indicated by 0 return
38        while ((bytesRead = netStream.Read(buffer, 0, buffer.Length)) > 0) {
39          totalBytesRead += bytesRead;
40
41          // Convert the incoming bytes to Unicode char array
42          int charCount = uniDecoder.GetCharCount(buffer, 0, bytesRead);
43          chars = new Char[charCount];
44          int charsDecodedCount = uniDecoder.GetChars(buffer, 0, bytesRead, chars, 0)
45
46          // Convert the Unicode char array to UTF8 bytes
47          int byteCount = Encoding.UTF8.GetByteCount(chars, 0, charsDecodedCount);
48          byte[] outputBuffer = new byte[byteCount];
49          Encoding.UTF8.GetBytes(chars, 0, charsDecodedCount, outputBuffer, 0);
50
51          // Send UTF8 bytes back to client
52          netStream.Write(outputBuffer, 0, outputBuffer.Length);
53          totalBytesWritten += outputBuffer.Length;
54        }
55
```

```
56          Console.WriteLine("Total bytes read:    {0}", totalBytesRead);
57          Console.WriteLine("Total bytes written: {0}", totalBytesWritten);
58          Console.WriteLine("Closing client connection...");
59
60          netStream.Close(); // Close the stream
61          client.Close();    // Close the socket
62        }
63      /* NOT REACHED */
64    }
65  }
```

TranscodeServer.cs

1. **Parameter parsing and socket setup:** lines 11–18

2. **Accept a connection and get the stream:** lines 24–29

3. **Initialize byte counters and encodings:** lines 31–35

4. **Loop until end of stream, performing:** lines 37–54
   - **Read network stream into buffer:** line 38
     Read up to the maximum buffer size bytes until 0 is returned indicating the Shutdown(SocketShutdown.Send) call was invoked by the client.
   - **Increment total bytes read:** line 39
   - **Convert Unicode to UTF-8:** lines 41–48
     Note that we are receiving data in the multibyte format (Unicode) over a medium that does not preserve message boundaries (TCP). This means that it is possible that a given read contains an odd number of bytes, creating an incomplete Unicode character at the end. Luckily, .NET provides a class for just such a situation. The Decoder class keeps state from one call to the next. Therefore if a call to GetChars() ends with an incomplete character, the bytes for that incomplete character are stored and added to the beginning of the next input to GetChars(). This allows us to process the stream data correctly regardless of where the message boundaries fall.
   - **Write the UTF-8 bytes out of the network stream:** line 52
   - **Increment total bytes written:** line 53

5. **Output results:** lines 56–58

6. **Close stream and socket:** lines 60–61

4.7 Wrapping Up

We have discussed some of the ways .NET provides access to advanced features of the sockets API, and how built-in features such as threads can be used with socket programs.

In addition to these facilities, .NET provides several mechanisms that operate on top of TCP or UDP and attempt to hide the complexity of protocol development. For example, *Remoting* allows .NET objects on different hosts to invoke one another's methods as if the objects all reside locally. Many other standard .NET library mechanisms exist, providing an amazing range of services. These mechanisms are beyond the scope of this book; however, we encourage you to look at the the Microsoft Developer Network site at *www.msdn.microsoft.com* for descriptions and code examples for some of these libraries.

4.8 Exercises

1. State precisely the conditions under which an iterative server is preferable to a multiprocessing server.

2. Would you ever need to implement a timeout in a client or server that uses TCP?

3. How can you determine the minimum and maximum allowable sizes for a socket's send and receive buffers? Determine the minimums for your system.

4. Write an iterative dispatcher using the dispatching framework from this chapter.

5. Write the server side of a random-number server using the protocol factory framework from this chapter. The client will connect and send the upper bound, *B*, on the random number to the server. The server should return a random number between 1 and *B*, inclusive. All numbers should be specified in binary format as 4-byte, two's-complement, big-endian integers.

6. Modify TcpEchoClient.cs so that it closes its output side of the connection before attempting to receive any echoed data.

7. Modify TcpEchoServerAsync.cs so that it polls for the accept to be completed after each sleep in the doOtherStuff() method (instead of waiting until each method call completes).

8. Modify some of the existing programs to implement asynchronous DNS lookups and asynchronous Connect().

chapter **5**

Under the Hood

Some of the subtleties of network programming are difficult to grasp without some understanding of the data structures associated with the socket implementation and certain details of how the underlying protocols work. This is especially true of TCP sockets (i.e., instances of TcpClient, TcpListener, or a TCP instance of Socket). This chapter describes some of what goes on in the runtime implementation when you create and use an instance of Socket or one of the higher level TCP classes that utilize sockets. Unless specifically stated otherwise, references to the behavior of the Socket class in this chapter also apply to TcpClient and TcpListener classes, which create Socket instances "under the hood." (The initial discussion and Section 5.2 apply as well to UdpClient). However, most of this chapter focuses on TCP sockets, that is, a TCP instance of Socket (whether used directly or indirectly via a higher level class). Please note that this description covers only the normal sequence of events and glosses over many details. Nevertheless, we believe that even this basic level of understanding is helpful. Readers who want the full story are referred to the TCP specification [12] or to one of the more comprehensive treatises on the subject [3, 20, 22].

Figure 5.1 is a simplified view of some of the information associated with a Socket instance. The classes are supported by an underlying implementation that is provided by the CLR and/or the platform on which it is running (i.e., the "socket layer" of the Windows operating system). Operations on the C# objects are translated into manipulations of this underlying abstraction. In this chapter, "Socket" refers generically to one of the classes in Figure 5.1, while "socket" refers to the underlying abstraction, whether it is provided by an underlying OS or the CLR implementation itself (e.g., in an embedded system). It is important to note that other (possibly non-C#/.NET) programs running on the same host may be using the network via the underlying socket abstraction and thus competing with C# Socket instances for resources such as ports.

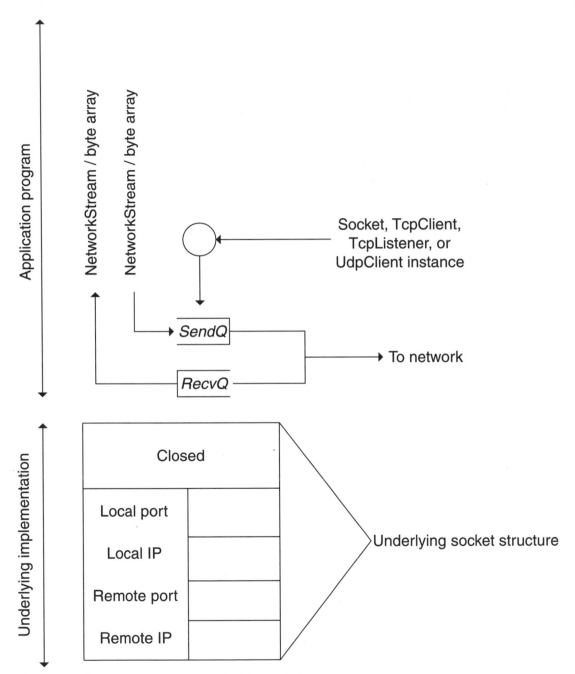

Figure 5.1: Data structures associated with a socket.

By "socket structure" here we mean the collection of data structures in the underlying implementation (of both the CLR and TCP/IP, but primarily the latter) that contain the information associated with a particular Socket instance. For example, the socket structure contains, among other information:

- The local and remote Internet addresses and port numbers associated with the socket. The local Internet address (labeled "Local IP" in Figure 5.1) is one of those assigned to the local host; the local port is set at Socket creation time. The remote address and port identify the remote socket, if any, to which the local socket is connected. We will say more about how and when these values are determined shortly (Section 5.5 contains a concise summary).

- A FIFO queue of received data waiting to be delivered and a queue for data waiting to be transmitted.

- For a TCP socket, additional protocol state information relevant to the opening and closing TCP handshakes. In Figure 5.1, the state is "Closed"; all sockets start out in the Closed state.

Knowing that these data structures exist and how they are affected by the underlying protocols is useful because they control various aspects of the behavior of the various Socket objects. For example, because TCP provides a *reliable* byte-stream service, a copy of any data written to a TcpClient's NetworkStream must be kept until it has been successfully received at the other end of the connection. Writing data to the network stream does *not* imply that the data has actually been sent, only that it has been copied into the local buffer. Even Flush()ing a NetworkStream doesn't guarantee that anything goes over the wire immediately. (This is also true for a byte array sent to a Socket instance.) Moreover, the nature of the byte-stream service means that message boundaries are *not* preserved in the network stream. As we saw in Section 3.3, this complicates the process of receiving and parsing for some protocols. On the other hand, with a UdpClient, packets are *not* buffered for retransmission, and by the time a call to the Send() method returns, the data has been given to the network subsystem for transmission. If the network subsystem cannot handle the message for some reason, the packet is silently dropped (but this is rare).

The next three sections deal with some of the subtleties of sending and receiving with TCP's byte-stream service. Then, Section 5.4 considers the connection establishment and termination of the TCP protocol. Finally, Section 5.5 discusses the process of matching incoming packets to sockets and the rules about binding to port numbers.

5.1 Buffering and TCP

As a programmer, the most important thing to remember when using a TCP socket is this:

> *You cannot assume any correspondence between writes to the output network stream at one end of the connection and reads from the input network stream at the other end.*

In particular, data passed in a single invocation of the output network stream's Write() method at the sender can be spread across multiple invocations of the input network stream's Read() method at the other end; and a single Read() may return data passed in multiple Write()s. To see this, consider a program that does the following:

```
byte[] buffer0 = new byte[1000];
byte[] buffer1 = new byte[2000];
byte[] buffer2 = new byte[5000];
    ⋮
TcpClient client = new TcpClient();
client.Connect(destAddr, destPort);
NetworkStream out = client.GetStream();
    ⋮
out.Write(buffer0);
    ⋮
out.Write(buffer1);
    ⋮
out.Write(buffer2);
    ⋮
out.Close();
```

where the ellipses represent code that sets up the data in the buffers but contains no other calls to out.Write(). Throughout this discussion, "in" refers to the incoming NetworkStream of the receiver's Socket, and "out" refers to the outgoing NetworkStream of the sender's Socket.

This TCP connection transfers 8000 bytes to the receiver. The way these 8000 bytes are grouped for delivery at the receiving end of the connection depends on the timing between the out.Write()s and in.Read()s at the two ends of the connection—as well as the size of the buffers provided to the in.Read() calls.

We can think of the sequence of all bytes sent (in one direction) on a TCP connection up to a particular instant in time as being divided into three FIFO queues:

1. *SendQ*: Bytes buffered in the underlying implementation at the sender that have been written to the output network stream but not yet successfully transmitted to the receiving host.

2. *RecvQ*: Bytes buffered in the underlying implementation at the receiver waiting to be delivered to the receiving program—that is, read from the input network stream.

3. *Delivered*: Bytes already read from the input network stream by the receiver.

A call to out.Write() at the sender appends bytes to *SendQ*. The TCP protocol is responsible for moving bytes—in order—from *SendQ* to *RecvQ*. It is important to realize that this transfer cannot be controlled or directly observed by the user program, and that it occurs in chunks whose sizes are more or less independent of the size of the buffers passed in Write()s. Bytes are moved from *RecvQ* to *Delivered* as they are read from the Socket's NetworkStream (or byte array) by the receiving program; the size of the transferred chunks depends on the amount of data in *RecvQ* and the size of the buffer given to Read().

Figure 5.2 shows one possible state of the three queues *after* the three out.Write()s in the example above, but *before* any in.Read()s at the other end. The different shading patterns denote bytes passed in the three different invocations of Write() shown in Figure 5.2.

Now suppose the receiver calls Read() with a byte array of size 2000. The Read() call will move all of the 1500 bytes present in the waiting-for-delivery (*RecvQ*) queue into the byte array and return the value 1500. Note that this data includes bytes passed in both the first and second calls to Write(). At some time later, after TCP has completed transfer of more data, the three partitions might be in the state shown in Figure 5.3.

If the receiver now calls Read() with a buffer of size 4000, that many bytes will be moved from the waiting-for-delivery (*RecvQ*) queue to the already-delivered (*Delivered*)

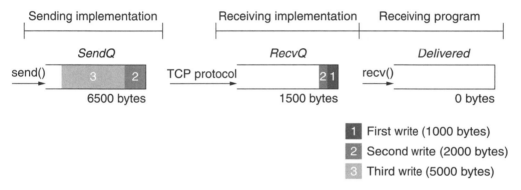

Figure 5.2: State of the three queues after three writes.

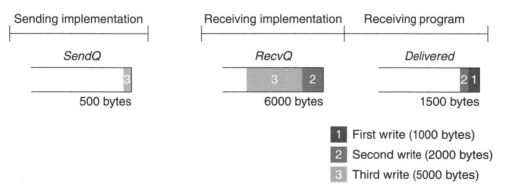

Figure 5.3: After first read().

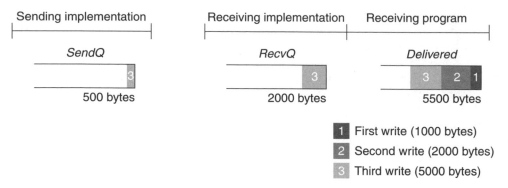

Figure 5.4: After another Read().

queue; this includes the remaining 1500 bytes from the second Write(), plus the first 2500 bytes from the third Write(). The resulting state of the queues is shown in Figure 5.4.

The number of bytes returned by the next call to Read() depends on the size of the buffer and the timing of the transfer of data over the network from the send-side socket/TCP implementation to the receive-side implementation. The movement of data from the *SendQ* to the *RecvQ* buffer has important implications for the design of application protocols. We have already encountered the need to parse messages as they are received via a Socket when in-band delimiters are used for framing (see Section 3.3). In the following sections, we consider two more subtle ramifications.

5.2 Buffer Deadlock

Application protocols have to be designed with some care to avoid *deadlock*—that is, a state in which each peer is blocked waiting for the other to do something. For example, it is pretty obvious that if both client and server try to do a blocking receive immediately after a connection is established, deadlock will result. Deadlock can also occur in less immediate ways.

The buffers *SendQ* and *RecvQ* in the implementation have limits on their capacity. Although the actual amount of memory they use may grow and shrink dynamically, a hard limit is necessary to prevent all of the system's memory from being gobbled up by a single TCP connection under control of a misbehaving program. Because these buffers are finite, they can fill up, and it is this fact, coupled with TCP's *flow control* mechanism, that leads to the possibility of another form of deadlock.

Once *RecvQ* is full, the TCP flow control mechanism kicks in and prevents the transfer of any bytes from the sending host's *SendQ*, until space becomes available in *RecvQ* as a result of the receiver calling the input network stream's Read() method. (The purpose of the flow control mechanism is to ensure that the sender does not transmit more data than the receiving system can handle.) A sending program can continue to call send until *SendQ* is full; however, once *SendQ* is full, a call to out.Write() will block until space becomes available, that is, until some bytes are transferred to the receiving socket's *RecvQ*. If *RecvQ* is also full, everything stops until the receiving program calls in.Read() and some bytes are transferred to *Delivered*.

Let's assume that the sizes of *SendQ* and *RecvQ* are *SQS* and *RQS*, respectively. A write() call with a byte array of size *n* such that $n > SQS$ will not return until at least $n - SQS$ bytes have been transferred to *RecvQ* at the receiving host. If *n* exceeds $(SQS + RQS)$, Write() cannot return until after the receiving program has read at least $n - (SQS + RQS)$ bytes from the input network stream. If the receiving program does not call Read(), a large Send() may not complete successfully. In particular, if both ends of the connection invoke their respective output network streams' Write() method simultaneously with buffers greater than $SQS + RQS$, deadlock will result: neither write will ever complete, and both programs will remain blocked forever.

As a concrete example, consider a connection between a program on Host A and a program on Host B. Assume *SQS* and *RQS* are 500 at both A and B. Figure 5.5 shows what happens when both programs try to send 1500 bytes at the same time. The first 500 bytes of data in the program at Host A have been transferred to the other end; another 500 bytes have been copied into *SendQ* at Host A. The remaining 500 bytes cannot be sent—and therefore out.Write() will not return—until space frees up in *RecvQ* at Host B. Unfortunately, the same situation holds in the program at Host B. Therefore, neither program's Write() call will ever complete.

The moral of the story: Design the protocol carefully to avoid sending large quantities of data simultaneously in both directions.

Can this really happen? Let's review the Transcode conversion protocol example in Section 4.6. Try running the Transcode client with a large file. The precise definition of

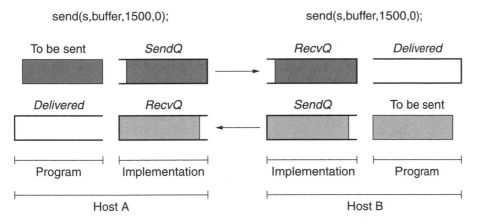

Figure 5.5: Deadlock due to simultaneous Write()s to output network streams at opposite ends of the connection.

"large" here depends on your system, but a file that exceeds 2MB should do nicely. For each read/write, the client prints an "R"/"W" to the console. If both the versions of the file are large enough (the UTF-8 version will be at a minimum half the size of the Unicode bytes sent by the client), your client will print a series of "Ws" and then stop without terminating or printing any "Rs."

Why does this happen? The program TranscodeClient.cs sends *all* of the Unicode data to the server *before* it attempts to read anything from the encoded stream. The server, on the other hand, simply reads the Unicode byte sequence and writes the UTF-8 sequence back to the client. Consider the case where *SendQ* and *RecvQ* for both client and server hold 500 bytes each and the client sends a 10,000-byte Unicode file. Let's assume that the file has no characters requiring double byte representation, so we know we will be sending half the number of bytes back. After the client sends 2000 bytes, the server will eventually have read them all and sent back 1000 bytes, and the client's *RecvQ* and the server's *SendQ* will both be full. After the client sends another 1000 bytes and the server reads them, the server's subsequent attempt to write will block. When the client sends the next 1000 bytes, the client's *SendQ* and the server's *RecvQ* will both fill up. The next client write will block, creating deadlock.

How do we solve this problem? The easiest solution is to execute the client writing and reading loop in separate threads. One thread repeatedly reads a buffer of Unicode bytes from a file and sends them to the server until the end of the file is reached, whereupon it calls Shutdown(SocketShutdown.Send) on the socket. The other thread repeatedly reads a buffer of UTF-8 bytes from the server and writes them to the output file, until the input network stream ends (i.e., the server closes the socket). When one thread blocks, the other thread can proceed independently. We can easily modify our client to follow this approach by putting the call to SendBytes() in TranscodeClient.cs inside a thread as follows:

```
Thread thread = new Thread(new ThreadStart(sendBytes));
thread.Start();
```

See TranscodeClientNoDeadlock.cs on the book's website (www.mkp.com/practical/csharpsockets) for the complete example of solving this problem with threads. Can we also solve this problem without using threads? To guarantee deadlock avoidance in a single threaded solution, we need nonblocking writes. Nonblocking writes are available via the Socket Blocking property or using the Socket BeginSend()/EndSend() methods or the NetworkStream BeginRead()/EndRead() methods.

5.3 Performance Implications

The TCP implementation's need to copy user data into *SendQ* for potential retransmission also has implications for performance. In particular, the sizes of the *SendQ* and *RecvQ* buffers affect the throughput achievable over a TCP connection. Throughput refers to the rate at which bytes of user data from the sender are made available to the receiving program; in programs that transfer a large amount of data, we want to maximize this rate.

In the absence of network capacity or other limitations, bigger buffers generally result in higher throughput.

The reason for this has to do with the cost of transferring data into and out of the buffers in the underlying implementation. If you want to transfer n bytes of data (where n is large), it is generally much more efficient to call Write() once with a buffer of size n than it is to call it n times with a single byte.[1] However, if you call Write() with a size parameter that is much larger than *SQS*, the system has to transfer the data from the user address space in *SQS*-sized chunks. That is, the socket implementation fills up the *SendQ* buffer, waits for data to be transferred out of it by the TCP protocol, refills *SendQ*, waits some more, and so on. Each time the socket implementation has to wait for data to be removed from *SendQ*, some time is wasted in the form of overhead (a context switch occurs). This overhead is comparable to that incurred by a completely new call to Write(). Thus, the *effective* size of a call to Write() is limited by the actual *SQS*. For reading from the Network-Stream/Socket, the same principle applies: however large the buffer we give to Read(), it will be copied out in chunks no larger than *RQS*, with overhead incurred between chunks.

If you are writing a program for which throughput is an important performance metric, you will want to change the send and receive buffer sizes using the Set-SocketOption() methods of Socket with SocketOptionName.SendBufferSize and Socket-OptionName.ReceiveBufferSize, or the SendBufferSize and ReceiveBufferSize() public properties of TcpClient. Although there is always a system-imposed maximum size for each buffer, it is typically significantly larger than the default on modern systems. Remember that these considerations apply only if your program needs to send an amount of data significantly larger than the buffer size, all at once. Note also that these factors may make little difference if the program deals with some higher-level stream derived from the Socket's basic network stream (say, by using it to create an instance of BufferedStream or BinaryWriter), which may perform its own internal buffering or add other overhead.

5.4 TCP Socket Life Cycle

When a new instance of the Socket class is connected—either via one of the Connect() calls or by calling one the Accept() methods of a Socket or TcpListener—it can immediately be used for sending and receiving data. That is, when the instance is returned, it is already connected to a remote peer and the opening TCP message exchange, or handshake, has been completed by the implementation.

Let us therefore consider in more detail how the underlying structure gets to and from the connected, or "Established," state; as you'll see later (in Section 5.4.2), these details affect the definition of reliability and the ability to create a Socket bound to a particular port.

---

[1]The same thing generally applies to reading data from the Socket, although calling Read()/Receive() with a larger buffer does not guarantee that more data will be returned.

5.4.1   Connecting

The relationship between an invocation of a TCP client connection (whether by TcpClient constructor, TcpClient.Connect(), or Socket.Connect()) and the protocol events associated with connection establishment at the client are illustrated in Figure 5.6. In this and the remaining figures in this section, the large arrows depict external events that cause the underlying socket structures to change state. Events that occur in the application program—that is, method calls and returns—are shown in the upper part of the figure; events such as message arrivals are shown in the lower part of the figure. Time proceeds left to right in these figures. The client's Internet address is depicted as A.B.C.D, while the server's is W.X.Y.Z; the server's port number is Q.

When the client calls the TcpClient constructor with the server's Internet address, W.X.Y.Z, and port, Q, the underlying implementation creates a socket instance; it is initially in the Closed state. If the client did not specify the local address and port number in the constructor call, a local port number (P), not already in use by another TCP socket, is chosen by the implementation. The local Internet address is also assigned; if not explicitly specified, the address of the network interface through which packets will be sent to the server is used. The implementation copies the local and remote addresses and ports into the underlying socket structure, and initiates the TCP connection establishment handshake.

The TCP opening handshake is known as a *3-way handshake* because it typically involves three messages: a connection request from client to server, an acknowledgment from server to client, and another acknowledgment from client back to server. The client TCP considers the connection to be established as soon as it receives the acknowledgment from the server. In the normal case, this happens quickly. However, the Internet is a best-effort network, and either the client's initial message or the server's response can get lost. For this reason, the TCP implementation retransmits handshake messages multiple times, at increasing intervals. If the client TCP does not receive a response from the server after some time, it *times out* and gives up. In this case the constructor throws a SocketException with the ErrorCode property set to 10060 (connection timed out). The connection timeout is generally long (by default 20 seconds on Microsoft Windows), and thus it can take some time for a TcpClient() constructor to fail. If the server is not accepting connections—say, if there is no program associated with the given port at the destination—the server-side TCP will send a rejection message instead of an acknowledgment, and the constructor will throw a SocketException almost immediately, with the ErrorCode property set to 10061 (connection refused).

The sequence of events at the server side is rather different; we describe it in Figures 5.7, 5.8, and 5.9. The server first creates an instance of TcpListener/Socket associated with its well-known port (here, Q). The socket implementation creates an underlying socket structure for the new TcpListener/Socket instance, and fills in Q as the local port and the special *wildcard address* ("*" in the figures, IPAddress.Any in C#) for the local IP address. (The server may also specify a local IP address in the constructor, but typically it does not. In case the server host has more than one IP address, not specifying the local address allows the socket to receive connections addressed to any of the server host's

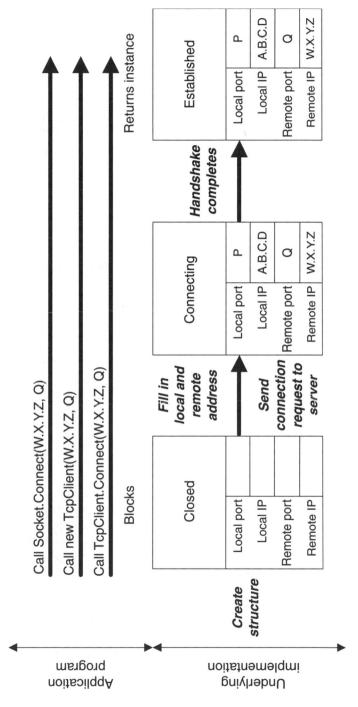

Figure 5.6: Client-side connection establishment.

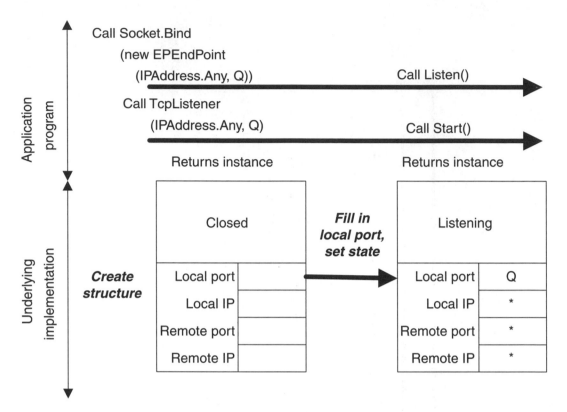

Figure 5.7: Server-side socket setup.

addresses.) After the call to `Start()` for `TcpListener` or `Listen()` for `Socket`, the state of the socket is set to "Listening," indicating that it is ready to accept incoming connection requests addressed to its port. This sequence is depicted in Figure 5.7.

The server can make the accept call (`Accept()` for `Socket` or either `AcceptSocket()` or `AcceptTcpClient()` for `TcpListener`, which will all be referred to collectively as `Accept*()` from here on) blocks until the TCP opening handshake has been completed with some client and a new connection has been established. We therefore focus in Figure 5.8 on the events that occur in the TCP implementation when a client connection request arrives. Note that everything depicted in this figure happens "under the covers," in the TCP implementation.

When the request for a connection arrives from the client, a new socket structure is created for the connection. The new socket's addresses are filled in based on the arriving packet: the packet's destination Internet address and port (W.X.Y.Z and Q, respectively) become the local Internet address and port; the packet's source address and port (A.B.C.D and P) become the remote Internet address and port. Note that the local port number of the new socket is always the same as that of the `TcpListener`. The new socket's state is set to "Connecting," and it is added to a list of not-quite-connected sockets associated with

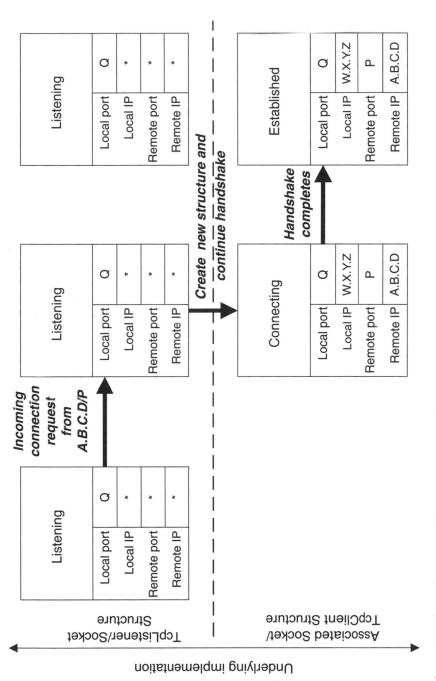

Figure 5.8: Incoming connection request processing.

the socket structure of the TcpListener. Note that the TcpListener itself does not change state, nor does any of its address information change.

In addition to creating a new underlying socket structure, the server-side TCP implementation sends an acknowledging TCP handshake message back to the client. However, the server TCP does not consider the handshake complete until the third message of the 3-way handshake is received from the client. When that message eventually arrives, the new structure's state is set to "Established," and it is then (and only then) moved to a list of socket structures associated with the TcpListener structure, which represent established connections ready to be Accept*()ed via the TcpListener. (If the third handshake message fails to arrive, eventually the "Connecting" structure is deleted.)

Now we can consider (in Figure 5.9) what happens when the server program calls the TcpListener/ Socket's Accept*() method. The call unblocks as soon as there is something in its associated list of socket structures for new connections. (Note that this list may already be nonempty when Accept*() is called.) At that time, one of the new connection structures is removed from the list, and an instance of Socket or TcpClient is created for it and returned as the result of the Accept*().

It is important to note that each structure in the TcpListener's associated list represents a fully established TCP connection with a client at the other end. Indeed, the client can send data as soon as it receives the second message of the opening handshake—which may be long before the server calls Accept*() to get a Socket instance for it.

5.4.2   Closing a TCP Connection

TCP has a *graceful close* mechanism that allows applications to terminate a connection without having to worry about loss of data that might still be in transit. The mechanism is also designed to allow data transfers in each direction to be terminated independently, as in the encoding example of Section 4.6. It works like this: the application indicates that it is finished sending data on a connected socket by calling Close() or by calling Shutdown(SocketShutdown.Send). At that point, the underlying TCP implementation first transmits any data remaining in *SendQ* (subject to available space in *RecvQ* at the other end), and then sends a closing TCP handshake message to the other end. This closing handshake message can be thought of as an end-of-transmission marker: it tells the receiving TCP that no more bytes will be placed in *RecvQ*. (Note that the closing handshake message itself is *not* passed to the receiving application, but that its position in the byte stream is indicated by Read() returning 0.) The closing TCP waits for an acknowledgment of its closing handshake message, which indicates that all data sent on the connection made it safely to *RecvQ*. Once that acknowledgment is received, the connection is "Half closed." It is not *completely* closed until a symmetric handshake happens in the other direction—that is, until *both* ends have indicated that they have no more data to send.

The closing event sequence in TCP can happen in two ways: either one application calls Close() (or Shutdown(SocketShutdown.Send)) and completes its closing handshake before the other calls Close(), or both call Close() simultaneously, so that their closing handshake messages cross in the network. Figure 5.10 shows the sequence of events in

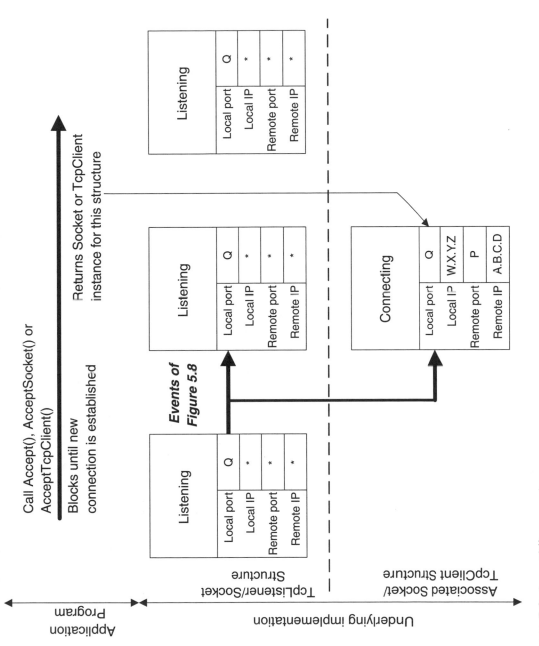

Figure 5.9: Accept*() processing.

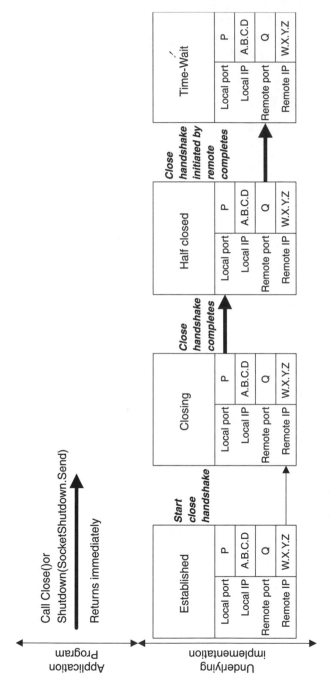

Figure 5.10: Closing a TCP connection first.

the implementation when the application invokes Close() *before* the other end closes. The closing handshake message is sent, the state of the socket structure is set to "Closing," and the call returns. After this point, further reads and writes on the Socket are disallowed (they throw an exception). When the acknowledgment for the close handshake is received, the state changes to "Half closed," where it remains until the other end's close handshake message is received. Note that if the remote endpoint goes away while the connection is in this state, the local underlying structure will stay around indefinitely. When the other end's close handshake message arrives, an acknowledgment is sent and the state is changed to "Time-Wait." Although the corresponding Socket instance in the application program may have long since vanished, the associated underlying structure continues to exist in the implementation for a minute or more; the reasons for this are discussed on page 164.

Figure 5.11 shows the simpler sequence of events at the endpoint that does not close first. When the closing handshake message arrives, an acknowledgment is sent immediately, and the connection state becomes "Close-Wait." At this point, we are just waiting for the application to invoke the Socket's Close() method. When it does, the final close handshake is initiated and the underlying socket structure is deallocated, although references to its original Socket instance may persist in the C# program.

In view of the fact that both Close() and Shutdown(SocketShutdown.Send) return without waiting for the closing handshake to complete, you may wonder how the sender

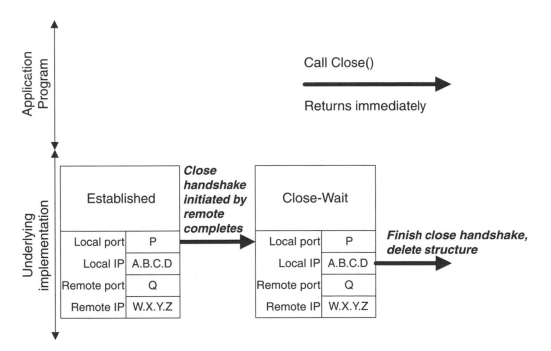

Figure 5.11: Closing after the other end closes.

can be assured that sent data has actually made it to the receiving program (i.e., to *Delivered*). In fact, it is possible for an application to call Close() or Shutdown(Socket-Shutdown.Send) and have it complete successfully (i.e., not throw an exception) *while there is still data in SendQ.* If either end of the connection then crashes before the data makes it to *RecvQ*, data may be lost without the sending application knowing about it.

The best solution is to design the application protocol so that the side that calls Close() first does so *only after* receiving application-level assurance that its data was received. For example, when our TCPEchoClient program receives the echoed copy of the data it sent, there should be nothing more in transit in either direction, so it is safe to close the connection.

.NET does provide a way to modify the behavior of the Socket's Close() method, namely by modifying the linger option. The linger option is accessed by either using the LingerState property of TcpClient class, or by Socket's Get/SetSocketOption() methods. In both cases the LingerOption class is used to control how long Close() waits for the closing handshake to complete before returning. The LingerOption class takes two parameters: a Boolean that indicates whether to wait, and an integer specifying the number of seconds to wait before giving up. That is, when a timeout is specified via LingerOption, Close() blocks until the closing handshake is completed, or until the specified amount of time passes.

Here is an example of setting the socket option:

```
sock.SetSocketOption(SocketOptionLevel.Socket,
                     SocketOptionName.Linger,
                     (object)new LingerOption(true, 10));
```

Here is an example of setting the TcpClient public LingerState property:

```
client.LingerState = new LingerOption(true, 10);
```

At the time of this writing, however, Close() provides no indication that the closing handshake failed to complete, even if the timelimit set by the LingerOption expires before the closing sequence completes. In other words, using the LingerOption may provide additional time, but does not provide any additional confirmation to the application in current implementations.

The final subtlety of closing a TCP connection revolves around the need for the Time-Wait state. The TCP specification requires that when a connection terminates, at least one of the sockets persists in the Time-Wait state for a period of time after both closing handshakes complete. This requirement is motivated by the possibility of messages being delayed in the network. If both ends' underlying structures go away as soon as both closing handshakes complete, and a *new* connection is immediately established between the same pair of socket addresses, a message from the previous connection, which happened to be delayed in the network, could arrive just after the new connection is established. Because it would contain the same source and destination addresses, the old message could be mistaken for a message belonging to the new connection, and its data might (incorrectly) be delivered to the application.

Unlikely though this scenario may be, TCP employs multiple mechanisms to prevent it, including the Time-Wait state. The Time-Wait state ensures that every TCP connection ends with a quiet time, during which no data is sent. The quiet time is supposed to be equal to twice the maximum amount of time a packet can remain in the network. Thus, by the time a connection goes away completely (i.e., the socket structure leaves the Time-Wait state and is deallocated) and clears the way for a new connection between the same pair of addresses, no messages from the old instance can still be in the network. In practice, the length of the quiet time is implementation dependent, because there is no real mechanism that limits how long a packet can be delayed by the network. Values in use range from 4 minutes down to 30 seconds or even shorter (4 minutes is the default on Microsoft Windows).

The most important consequence of Time-Wait is that as long as the underlying socket structure exists, no other socket is permitted to be associated with the same local port. In particular, any attempt to create a Socket instance using that port will throw a SocketException with a ErrorCode of 10048 (address already in use).

5.5 Demultiplexing Demystified

The fact that different sockets on the same machine can have the same local address and port number is implicit in the preceding discussions. For example, on a machine with only one IP address, every new Socket or TcpClient instance Accept()ed via a server Socket or TcpListener will have the same local port number as the server socket. Clearly the process of deciding to which socket an incoming packet should be delivered—that is, the *demultiplexing* process—involves looking at more than just the packet's destination address and port. Otherwise there could be ambiguity about which socket an incoming packet is intended for. The process of matching an incoming packet to a socket is actually the same for both TCP and UDP, and can be summarized by the following points:

- The local port in the socket structure *must* match the destination port number in the incoming packet.

- Any address fields in the socket structure that contain the wildcard value (*) are considered to match *any* value in the corresponding field in the packet.

- If there is more than one socket structure that matches an incoming packet for all four address fields, the one that matches using the fewest wildcards gets the packet.

For example, consider a host with two IP addresses, 10.1.2.3 and 192.168.3.2, and with a subset of its active TCP socket structures, as shown in Figure 5.12. The structure labeled 0 is associated with a TcpListener and has port 99 with a wildcard local address. Socket structure 1 is also for a TcpListener on the same port, but with the local IP address 10.1.2.3 specified (so it will only accept connection requests to that address). Structure 2 is for a connection that was accepted via the TcpListener for structure 0, and thus has the same local port number, but also has its local and remote Internet addresses

Listening		Listening		Established		...	Established	
Local port	99	Local port	99	Local port	99		Local port	1025
Local IP	*	Local IP	10.1.2.3	Local IP	192.168.3.2		Local IP	10.1.2.3
Remote port	*	Remote port	*	Remote port	30001		Remote port	25
Remote IP	*	Remote IP	*	Remote IP	172.16.1.9		Remote IP	10.5.5.8
0		1		2				

Figure 5.12: Demultiplexing with multiple matching sockets.

filled in. Other sockets belong to other active connections. Now consider a packet with source IP address 172.16.1.10, source port 56789, destination IP address 10.1.2.3, and destination port 99. It will be delivered to the socket associated with structure 1, because that one matches with the fewest wildcards.

When a program attempts to create a socket with a particular local port number, the existing sockets are checked to make sure that no socket is already using that local port. A Socket Bind() will throw an exception if *any* socket matches the local port and local IP address (if any) specified. This can cause problems in the following scenario:

1. A client program creates a Socket with a specific local port number, say, *P*, and uses it to communicate with a server.

2. The client closes the Socket, and the underlying structure goes into the Time-Wait state.

3. The client program terminates and is immediately restarted.

If the new incarnation of the client attempts to use the same local port number, the Socket constructor will throw an SocketException with an ErrorCode of 10048 (address already in use), because of the other structure in the Time-Wait state.[2] One way to circumvent this problem is to wait until the underlying structure leaves the Time-Wait state. However, .NET also permits overriding this behavior by setting the ReuseAddress socket option, but this is only accessible via the Socket class and not any of the higher level classes:

```
sock.SetSocketOption(SocketOptionLevel.Socket,
                     SocketOptionName.ReuseAddress, 1);
```

So what determines the local/foreign address/port? For a TcpListener, all constructors require that the local port be specified. The local address may be specified to the constructor; otherwise, the local address is the wildcard (*) address. The foreign address

---

[2]Another scenario that does not require a convergence of several events to encounter this problem is several multicast receiver clients running on the same host.

and port for a TcpListener are always wildcards. For a TcpClient, all constructors require specification of the foreign address and port. The local address and/or port may be specified to the constructor.[3] Otherwise, the local address is the address of the network interface through which the connection to the server is established, and the local port is a randomly selected, unused port number greater than 1023. For a Socket or TcpClient instance returned by an Accept(), AcceptSocket(), or AcceptTcpClient() call, the local address is the destination address from the initial handshake message from the client, the local port is the local port of the server (Socket or TcpListener), and the foreign address/port is the local address/port of the client. For a UdpClient, the local address and/or port may be specified to the constructor. Otherwise, the local address is the wildcard address, and the local port is a randomly selected, unused port number greater than 1023. The foreign address and port are initially both wildcards and remain that way unless the Connect() method is invoked to specify particular values.

5.6 Exercises

1. The TCP protocol is designed so that simultaneous connection attempts will succeed. That is, if an application using port P and Internet address W.X.Y.Z attempts to connect to address A.B.C.D, port Q, at the same time as an application using the same address and port tries to connect to W.X.Y.Z, port P, they will end up connected to each other. Can this be made to happen when the programs use the sockets API?

2. The first example of "buffer deadlock" in this chapter involves the programs on both ends of a connection trying to send large messages. However, this is not necessary for deadlock. How could the TCPEchoClient from Chapter 2 be made to deadlock when it connects to the TCPEchoServer from that chapter?

3. Write a version of UnicodeClientNoDeadlock using nonblocking writes (BeginSend() and EndSend()).

---

[3]This is true for the higher level .NET socket classes but not for the .NET Socket class itself.

Handling Socket Errors

Most of the socket constructors and methods in the .NET library can throw a Socket-Exception. Unlike some other exception classes in the .NET library, the SocketException class is fairly generic and requires some additional work to find out what type of error occurred. SocketException contains two useful properties, Message and ErrorCode. The Message property contains a human-readable error message. The ErrorCode property contains a WinSock error code from the underlying implementation, and can be used to trap and handle very specific error conditions.

Table A.1 lists the WinSock error codes that can be retrieved from the ErrorCode property. The Error Name field is the header constant used with WinSock. These constants are not accessible within C#, but it is useful to know the constant names because they are often referenced in WinSock documentation. This table is just a quick reference for convenience; you should refer to the Microsoft documentation on WinSock error codes at *www.msdn.microsoft.com* for more detailed information.

Error Name	Value	Description
WSAEINTR	10004	Interrupted function call.
WSAEACCES	10013	Permission denied.
WSAEFAULT	10014	Bad address.
WSAEINVAL	10022	Invalid argument.
WSAEMFILE	10024	Too many open files.
WSAEWOULDBLOCK	10035	Resource temporarily unavailable.
WSAEINPROGRESS	10036	Operation now in progress.
WSAEALREADY	10037	Operation already in progress.

Table A.1: Continued

Error Name	Value	Description
WSAENOTSOCK	10038	Socket operation on nonsocket.
WSAEDESTADDRREQ	10039	Destination address required.
WSAEMSGSIZE	10040	Message too long.
WSAEPROTOTYPE	10041	Protocol wrong type for socket.
WSAENOPROTOOPT	10042	Bad protocol option.
WSAEPROTONOSUPPORT	10043	Protocol not supported.
WSAESOCKTNOSUPPORT	10044	Socket type not supported.
WSAEOPNOTSUPP	10045	Operation not supported.
WSAEPFNOSUPPORT	10046	Protocol family not supported.
WSAEAFNOSUPPORT	10047	Address family not supported by protocol family.
WSAEADDRINUSE	10048	Address already in use.
WSAEADDRNOTAVAIL	10049	Cannot assign requested address.
WSAENETDOWN	10050	Network is down.
WSAENETUNREACH	10051	Network is unreachable.
WSAENETRESET	10052	Network dropped connection on reset.
WSAECONNABORTED	10053	Software caused connection abort.
WSAECONNRESET	10054	Connection reset by peer.
WSAENOBUFS	10055	No buffer space available.
WSAEISCONN	10056	Socket is already connected.
WSAENOTCONN	10057	Socket is not connected.
WSAESHUTDOWN	10058	Cannot send after socket shutdown.
WSAETIMEDOUT	10060	Connection timed out.
WSAECONNREFUSED	10061	Connection refused.
WSAEHOSTDOWN	10064	Host is down.
WSAEHOSTUNREACH	10065	No route to host.
WSAEPROCLIM	10067	Too many processes.
WSASYSNOTREADY	10091	Network subsystem is unavailable.
WSAVERNOTSUPPORTED	10092	Winsock.dll version out of range.
WSANOTINITIALIZED	10093	Successful WSAStartup not yet performed.
WSAEDISCON	10101	Graceful shutdown in progress.
WSATYPE_NOT_FOUND	10109	Class type not found.
WSAHOST_NOT_FOUND	11001	Host not found.
WSATRY_AGAIN	11002	Nonauthoritative host not found.
WSANO_RECOVERY	11003	This is a nonrecoverable error.
WSANO_DATA	11004	Valid name, no data record of requested type.
WSA_INVALID_HANDLE	OS dependent	Specified event object handle is invalid.
WSA_INVALID_PARAMETER	OS dependent	One or more parameters are invalid.
WSA_IO_INCOMPLETE	OS dependent	Overlapped I/O event object not in signaled state.
WSA_IO_PENDING	OS dependent	Overlapped operations will complete later.
WSA_NOT_ENOUGH_MEMORY	OS dependent	Insufficient memory available.
WSA_OPERATION_ABORTED	OS dependent	Overlapped operation aborted.
WSAINVALIDPROCTABLE	OS dependent	Invalid procedure table from service provider.
WSAINVALIDPROVIDER	OS dependent	Invalid service provider version number.
WSAPROVIDERFAILEDINIT	OS dependent	Unable to initialize a service provider.
WSASYSCALLFAILURE	OS dependent	System call failure.

Table A.1: WinSock Error Codes

Bibliography

[1] Case, J. D., Fedor, M., and Schoffstall, M. L. "Simple Network Management Protocol (SNMP)." Internet Request for Comments 1157, May 1990.

[2] Comer, Douglas E. *Internetworking with TCP/IP,* volume 1, *Principles, Protocols, and Architecture* (third edition). Upper Saddle River, NJ: Prentice-Hall, 1995.

[3] Comer, Douglas E., and Stevens, David L. *Internetworking with TCP/IP,* volume 2, *Design, Implementation, and Internals* (third edition). Upper Saddle River, NJ: Prentice-Hall, 1999.

[4] Comer, Douglas E., and Stevens, David L. *Internetworking with TCP/IP,* volume 3, *Client-Server Programming and Applications* (BSD version, second edition). Upper Saddle River, NJ: Prentice-Hall, 1996.

[5] Deering, S., and Hinden, R. "Internet Protocol, Version 6 (IPv6) Specification." Internet Request for Comments 2460, December 1998.

[6] Gilligan, R., Thomson, S., Bound, J., and Stevens, W. "Basic Socket Interface Extensions for IPv6." Internet Request for Comments 2553, March 1999.

[7] International Organization for Standardization. *Basic Encoding Information Processing Systems: Open Systems Interconnection—Specification of Abstract Syntax Notation One (ASN.1).* International Standard 8824, December 1987.

[8] Mockapetris, Paul. "Domain Names: Concepts and Facilities." Internet Request for Comments 1034, November 1987.

[9] Mockapetris, Paul. "Domain Names: Implementation and Specification." Internet Request for Comments 1035, November 1987.

[10] Peterson, Larry L., and Davie, Bruce S. *Computer Networks: A Systems Approach* (second edition). San Francisco: Morgan Kaufmann, 2000.

[11] Postel, John. "Internet Protocol." Internet Request for Comments 791, September 1981.

[12] Postel, John. "Transmission Control Protocol." Internet Request for Comments 793, September 1981.

[13] Postel, John. "User Datagram Protocol." Internet Request for Comments 768, August 1980.

[14] Steedman, Douglas. *Abstract Syntax Notation One (ASN.1): The Tutorial and Reference.* London, U.K.: Technology Appraisals, 1990.

[15] Stevens, W. Richard. *TCP/IP Illustrated,* volume 1, *The Protocols.* Reading, MA: Addison-Wesley, 1994.

[16] Stevens, W. Richard. *UNIX Network Programming: Networking APIs: Sockets and XTI* (second edition). Upper Saddle River, NJ: Prentice-Hall, 1997.

[17] Sun Microsystems, Incorporated. "External Data Representation Standard." Internet Request for Comments 1014, June 1987.

[18] Sun Microsystems, Incorporated. "Network File System Protocol Specification." Internet Request for Comments 1094, March 1989.

[19] Sun Microsystems, Incorporated. "Network File System Protocol Version 3 Specification." Internet Request for Comments 1813, June 1995.

[20] Wright, Gary R., and Stevens, W. Richard. *TCP/IP Illustrated,* volume 2, *The Implementation.* Reading, MA: Addison-Wesley, 1995.

[21] Krowczyk, A., Kumar, V., Laghari, N., Mungale, A., Nagel, C., Parker, T., and Sivakumar, S. *.NET Network Programming.* Birmingham, U.K.: Wrox Press Ltd, 2002.

[22] Quinn, B., and Shute, D. *Windows Sockets Network Programming.* Reading, MA: Addison-Wesley, 1995.

[23] The Unicode Consortium. *The Unicode Standard, Version 3.* Reading, MA: Addison-Wesley, Longman, 2000.

[24] Donahoo, M., and Calvert, K. *TCP/IP Sockets in C: Practical Guide for Programmers.* San Francisco: Morgan Kaufmann, 2001.

[25] Calvert, K., and Donahoo, M. *TCP/IP Sockets in Java: Practical Guide for Programmers.* San Francisco: Morgan Kaufmann, 2002.

[26] Makofske, D., and Almeroth, K. *Multicast Sockets: Practical Guide for Programmers.* San Francisco: Morgan Kaufmann, 2002.

[27] Braden, R. "Requirements for Internet Hosts—Communications Layers." Internet Request for Comments 1122, October 1989.

[28] Braden, R. "Requirements for Internet Hosts—Application and Support." Internet Request for Comments 1123, October 1989.

Index